101 Answers
to Questions About
Satan, Demons, & Spiritual Warfare

Mark Hitchcock

HARVEST HOUSE PUBLISHERS
EUGENE, OREGON

Scripture quotations are taken from the New American Standard Bible®, © 1960, 1962, 1963, 1968, 1971, 1972, 1973, 1975, 1977, 1995 by The Lockman Foundation. Used by permission. (www.Lockman.org)

All italicized emphasis in Scripture quotations is added by the author.

Cover by Left Coast Design, Portland, Oregon

Cover photo © Dorottya Mathe / Shutterstock

101 ANSWERS TO QUESTIONS ABOUT SATAN, DEMONS, AND SPIRITUAL WARFARE
Copyright © 2014 by Mark Hitchcock
Published by Harvest House Publishers
Eugene, Oregon 97402
www.harvesthousepublishers.com

Library of Congress Cataloging-in-Publication Data
   Hitchcock, Mark, 1959-
   101 answers to questions about satan, demons, and spiritual warfare / Mark Hitchcock.
      pages cm
   ISBN 978-0-7369-4517-2 (pbk.)
   ISBN 978-0-7369-4518-9 (eBook)
   1. Devil—Miscellanea. 2. Demonology—Miscellanea. 3. Spiritual warfare—Miscellanea.
   I. Title. II. Title: One hundred and one answers to questions about satan, demons, and spiritual warfare. III. Title: One hundred one answers to questions about satan, demons, and spiritual warfare.
   BT982.H58 2014
   235'.4—dc23

                                        2013024776

Printed in the United States of America

        14 15 16 17 18 19 20 21 22 / VP-JH / 10 9 8 7 6 5 4 3 2 1

To Philip De Courcy,
whose infectious passion for Christ
and compelling preaching of God's Word
has forged a bond of friendship between us
that has blessed my life and ministry immeasurably

Contents

Introduction

Behind the *Seen*

There are two equal and opposite errors into which our race can fall about the devils. One is to disbelieve in their existence. The other is to believe, and to feel an excessive and unhealthy interest in them. They themselves are equally pleased by both errors, and hail a materialist or a magician with the same delight.

C.S. LEWIS

1

Why spend time thinking about Satan and demons?

As a chess master walked through an art gallery in Europe, he came across a painting that fascinated him. In it, a young man was playing a game of chess with the devil. There was a look of glee on the face of the enemy and of panic on the face of the young man. The name of the painting was *Checkmate*.

As the chess master observed the painting, he felt uncomfortable—something about the painting just wasn't right. He called for the curator of the gallery and asked him to take the painting down. When that didn't work, he requested to meet the artist. The artist agreed to meet him at the gallery.

The chess master arrived at the meeting with a chessboard and the chess pieces. He set up the board exactly as the artist had arranged it in the painting and said, "Something is wrong with your painting." When the artist inquired as to what that might be, the master stated, "You titled the painting *Checkmate*, but that implies that the young man has no more moves to make." The champion reached over to the board and moved the young man's king one space and said, "The devil is now checkmated." He then looked at the young man in the painting and said, "Young man, your enemy made a fatal miscalculation. You don't have to lose. You win!"[1]

Maybe you feel like the man in the painting sometimes. Maybe right now. Perhaps you picked up this book because you're in the struggle right now and are searching for answers. Fear and anxiety are stalking you night and day as you imagine the devil making the final move in your life. You feel as if you're about to be checkmated by struggles in your marriage, finances, career, health, or any of a myriad of other problems.

I've got great news. If you have trusted in Jesus Christ as your Savior, you win! Your Champion has defeated the enemy. The King made His final move and announced "checkmate" through His resurrection from the dead. The war has already been won. All you and I have to do is play out the rest of the game under His guiding hand and claim our victory in Him. In the battle against our enemy, God's people fight *from* victory, not *for* victory. Contrary to what many people might think, spiritual warfare is not scary or frightening. Understanding it brings us hope, encouragement, and reassurance that victory is ours through our Lord Jesus Christ.

Another reason why we should learn about spiritual warfare and the unseen world around us is simply that God has chosen to reveal it to us. This alone justifies our interest in the topic and the time we spend studying it. If God in His Word has defined, described, and delineated the spirit world behind the veil of the seen, it is incumbent on us to take this revelation seriously.

The study of systematic theology includes separate categories for the study of Satan and the study of demons. The study of Satan is called Satanology, and the study of demons is called demonology. These two areas are often combined. But the fact that entire areas of theology are devoted to these subjects should pique our interest.

As we will see in this book, the Bible includes a great deal about Satan, demons, and the unseen global conspiracy raging around us. Satan is mentioned for the first time in Genesis 3 and makes his inglorious exit in Revelation 20. It is not an overstatement to say that one cannot really understand the Bible from beginning to end without some knowledge of Satan and his evil minions. God has chosen to reveal truth to us about the unseen world from Genesis to Revelation, so it must be important for us to know about it.

A third reason to spend time thinking about spiritual warfare is that many different views of this topic exist. Champions of the modern-day spiritual warfare movement advocate cosmic-level spiritual warfare, spiritual mapping, and identifying and confronting territorial spirits. Many others promote deliverance ministry, including rebuking and binding Satan and demonic spirits. Are these practices biblical? Should believers participate in these activities? What does Scripture say? With the emergence of divergent views and practices, followers of Christ today need to understand what Scripture says about spiritual warfare in order to avoid being sidetracked by unbiblical practices and ending up on the casualty list. Spiritual warfare is not a game. Successful warfare against the enemy must be waged according to God's power and God's principles.

A fourth motivation for studying Satan, demons, and spiritual warfare is that according to Scripture, demonic activity and spiritual warfare will increase dramatically in frequency and intensity during the end times (see Revelation 9). We aren't in the end times yet, but we can expect demonic activity to ramp up as the end times draw near, and it appears that's just what's happening. With demonic activity increasing in intensity, we don't want our understanding and awareness of the unseen war to be on the decrease. That's a dangerous combination. Our study of spiritual warfare must match its surge in our world today. We cannot afford to be disarmed.

A fifth motivation for us to understand the unseen world around us is that it helps us make sense out of what we can see. According to the Bible, an invisible world war is raging all around us. Understanding this war gives us a unique perspective that those without this knowledge do not possess. Ray Stedman gives powerful insight into why we need to understand the spiritual war that surrounds us. Read this quote carefully.

As the world's great leaders grapple with the dilemma of modern life, all they can say is, "What is wrong? What is the unknown element behind this? We cannot understand or explain this! Something is missing from our understanding of human nature and human behavior. What is it?"

The answer: There is a spiritual war going on behind the scenes of history, and that spiritual war in the unseen world is driving events in our own visible world. There is no peace in the material world because there is a war now raging in the spiritual world.

There is nothing more meaningful, more relevant, more real that we could be involved in than the cause of God in this vast spiritual war. The biblical teaching of spiritual warfare shines a spotlight of truth on the basic problem of human existence and human history...

"Well," you say, "this is all very depressing. I would rather not think about it." I don't like to think about it either, but I have discovered that you cannot wish the truth away. There is only one realistic approach to this struggle, and this is to be strong in the Lord and in the power of his might...

Those who ignore this call and the battle that rages around them are doomed to be casualties. We cannot remain neutral. We must choose sides. We must align ourselves with the forces of God, the forces of good.[2]

Understanding this invisible war helps us to see the world as it really is. One of the fundamental truths of God's Word is that behind the paper-thin facade of this world, an invisible, relentless battle is raging. Satan is locked and loaded, and his bullets have our names on them. If we don't want to end up on the casualty list, we have to understand this battle and arm ourselves with God's powerful resources. The enemy has us in his crosshairs.

I once saw a *Far Side* cartoon of two deer standing next to one another. One of the deer is looking down at a bull's-eye on his stomach. The other deer says, "Bummer of a birthmark, Hal." Whether we like it or not, if we are seeking to live for Christ and His glory, we have bull's-eyes on us.

My friend Pastor Philip De Courcy told me a story that he heard Jill Briscoe relate to a group a few years ago. She was on her way back to the United States on September 11, 2001, from overseas. When the terrorists struck, her plane was diverted to Reykjavík, Iceland, where the crew and passengers had to spend a couple of days before they could continue their trip.

While in the airport Jill Briscoe observed a young female American soldier. She looked distressed and shaken. Jill Briscoe eventually initiated a conversation with her to see if she was okay, and try to encourage or comfort her. The young lady was shaken over the events of 9/11. When asked what had shaken her so deeply, the young woman, anticipating what was in her future, responded, "I didn't join the army to go to war."

Many believers are like that young soldier today. They didn't sign up to go to war. Many don't even want to think about it. But the truth is, every Christian must go to war. We have no choice, so we'd better make sure we know the enemy's strategy and have our armor on.

Our enemy is relentless and always probing for an opening.

Sir William Slim was a commander in the British Army who served with distinction in both World Wars and was wounded three times. When he was once asked where he learned his greatest lesson as a solider, he told a story that's so simple yet crucial that it's repeated today in the training manuals of the US Marine Corps.

> Many years ago as a cadet hoping someday to be an officer, I was poring over the "Principles of War," listed in the old Field Service Regulations, when the

Sergeant-Major came up to me. He surveyed me with kindly amusement. "Don't bother your head about all them things, me lad. There's only one principle of war and that's this. Hit the other fellow, as quick as you can, and as hard as you can, where it hurts him most, when he ain't lookin."[3]

Satan employs this sinister strategy against God's people every day.

Of course, our thinking about spiritual warfare requires careful balance. We don't want to go overboard and become obsessed with Satanology and demonology. Believers can be led to ignore the enemy on one hand or become too focused on Satan on the other. Either extreme is harmful, and the enemy doesn't care which extreme we adopt. To ignore Satan and his strategies is to commit spiritual suicide. But to become preoccupied with Satan and his kingdom is equally dangerous. A.W. Tozer highlights the danger of too much focus on Satan by calling Christians to keep Christ at the center of all things.

> The scriptural way to see things is to set the Lord always before us, put Christ in the center of our vision, and if Satan is lurking around he will appear on the margin only and be seen as but a shadow on the edge of the brightness. It is always wrong to reverse this—to set Satan in the focus of our vision and push God out to the margin. Nothing but tragedy can come of such inversion.
>
> The best way to keep the enemy out is to keep Christ in. The sheep need not be terrified by the wolf; they have but to stay close to the shepherd. It is not the praying sheep Satan fears, but the presence of the shepherd.

The instructed Christian whose faculties have been developed by the Word and the Spirit will not fear the devil. When necessary he will stand against the powers of darkness and overcome them by the blood of the Lamb and the word of his testimony. He will recognize the peril in which he lives and will know what to do about it, but he will practice the presence of God and never allow himself to become devil-conscious. [4]

We need to remember that in Paul's letters, he uses the word "Satan" only ten times and "devil" only six times. Conversely, we find the words "Jesus" in 219 verses, "Lord" in 272 verses, and "Christ" in 389 verses. Clearly, we are to rivet our attention on Christ, not Satan. We're to be Christ-centered, not Satan-centered.

May God help us to keep this balance in mind as we make our way through this book together. May our focus be on Christ our Conqueror, not our defeated enemy. Revelation 5:5-7 tells us that the Lamb who was slain is standing at the center of everything in heaven. If the crucified, resurrected Lamb is the focal point of heaven, how much more should He be the focus of everything here on earth—our churches, our families, our marriages, and our lives. Let's not allow our focus to be diverted from our dear Lamb, who was slain for us. Our focus should be on worship, not on warfare.

Our attitude toward our spiritual enemies should be like a quarterback's appreciation of an opponent's stout defense. If the quarterback keeps his eye on the linebackers and defensive backs, he will never connect with his receivers. The quarterback must focus primarily on his own backs and wide receivers, but at the same time he must be keenly aware of the defensive players and anticipate their moves, or his throw will be intercepted. The effective quarterback must carefully study the opponent's formations by watching hours of film. But when the game begins, his ultimate focus must be on his own assignments and his own receivers. That's the way we're to be when it comes to the subject of spiritual warfare. Our ultimate focus is on Christ and His game plan for our lives. But we are fools if we are ignorant of the devil and his schemes.

Part 1

Speak of the Devil

Satan promises the best, but pays with the worst; he promises honour and pays with disgrace; he promises pleasure and pays with pain; he promises profit and pays with loss; he promises life and pays with death.

THOMAS BROOKS

The Devil takes no holiday; he never rests. If beaten, he rises again. If he cannot enter in front, he steals in the rear. If he cannot enter at the rear, he breaks through the roof or enters by tunneling under the threshold. He labors until he is in. He uses great cunning and many a plan. When one miscarries, he has another at hand and continues in his attempts until he wins.

MARTIN LUTHER

2

Does Satan really exist?

A bruised and bleeding boxer stumbled back to his corner after a tough round. His trainer splashed cold water on his head and rubbed him down as his manager tried to encourage him. He said, "Rocky, you're doing great. Your opponent hasn't laid a glove on you."

The half-dazed boxer looked up and said, "If my opponent hasn't laid a glove on me, you'd better keep an eye on the referee because somebody out there is beating the daylights out of me."[1]

I think of that story when people question the reality of Satan. If the devil isn't real, then someone else like him is continually assaulting us. How else can we explain the extent of evil in the world? Make no mistake. Satan is real. He may rarely be recognized, and his existence may often be denied, but he is real. The Bible is full of references to him, and God's Word is our only reliable source for information about Satan, demons, and spiritual warfare. As E.M. Bounds notes, "The Bible is a revelation, not a philosophy or a poem, not a science. It reveals things and persons as they are, living and acting outside the range of earthly vision or natural discovery. Biblical revelations are not against reason but above reason."[2] Biblical revelation unveils the reality of an evil being named Satan.

The Bible refers to Satan by many names and titles. He is mentioned in seven of the thirty-nine Old Testament books—Genesis, 1 Chronicles, Job (12 times), Psalms, Isaiah, Ezekiel, and Zechariah. The most detailed passage about Satan in the Old Testament is Job 1–2, which may be the first inspired words ever recorded because most scholars believe Job was the first book of the Bible to be written. Satan stands before God in Job 1–2 with the other angels and speaks with Him directly. Genesis also presents the devil as a real being. C. Fred Dickason examines the evidence just from Genesis and Job for Satan's existence.

> The Old Testament assumes the existence of Satan, much as it does the existence of God. There is no formal proof presented for either one, but the story unfolds depending for its vitality upon their reality.
>
> The whole plot of the book of Genesis depends upon the reality of Satan working through the serpent to cause the fall of mankind into sin (chap. 3). The basic facts of the Creation and the fall lay the foundation for the whole battle between good and evil throughout the Bible and history, and for the whole redemptive plan of God centered in the God-man who overcomes Satan.
>
> The whole story of the tragedy and triumph of Job is based in the first two chapters upon the personal challenges and battle between God and Satan…
>
> We conclude that there are some books in the Old Testament that make little sense historically and exegetically without the reality of Satan's existence and influence as a person.[3]

Turning to the New Testament, Satan is recognized by every New Testament writer, although not in every book. Satan is mentioned in 19 of the 27 New Testament books, including 29 times in the Gospels, with 25 of those from the lips of Christ.

It is clear from the pages of Scripture from Genesis to Revelation that Satan exists. However, one of his subtlest yet strongest tactics is to convince people he doesn't exist. God desires above all to be fully believed and worshipped, but Satan, the master deceiver, works best when he is underestimated, ignored, or denied. As Vance Havner said, "God is the Great I AM. Satan is the great 'I am not'; and he is never happier than when he has convinced people that he is non-existent."[4] Satan loves to downplay his own existence so he can go about his business unheeded, unhindered, and unchecked. Those who don't believe he exists are playing right into his hands.

3

Is Satan a real person or just an impersonal force?

My sons and I love to watch old reruns of *The Twilight Zone*. Every year, one cable channel runs them nonstop for 24 hours. One of our favorites is an episode from 1960 that opens with an American hiking through Central Europe and getting caught in a raging storm. Staggering through the blinding rain, he sees an imposing medieval castle, which is a hermitage for a brotherhood of monks. The reclusive monks reluctantly take him in.

Later that night, the American discovers a cell with a man locked inside. An ancient wooden staff bolts the door. The prisoner claims he is being held captive by the insane head monk, Brother Jerome. He pleads for the American to release him.

The prisoner's kind face and gentle voice win over the American. The American confronts Brother Jerome, who tells him the prisoner is Satan, the father of lies, held captive by the Staff of Truth, the one barrier he cannot pass. That convinces the American that Jerome must be mad. As soon as he gets his chance, he releases the prisoner—who immediately transforms into a hideous horned demon and vanishes in a puff of smoke.

The stunned American is horrified by what he has done.

Jerome responds sympathetically. "I'm sorry for you, my son. All your life you will remember this night and whom you have turned loose upon the world."

"I didn't believe you," the American replies. "I saw him and didn't recognize him."

Brother Jerome responds, "That is man's weakness and Satan's strength." [1]

Scripture informs us that Satan exists, and it is equally clear that he is a real person—a real being—not just an impersonal force, such as gravity or electricity. Satan is not just a nebulous dark power but an evil fiend. In Scripture he possesses the essential traits of personality—intellect, emotion, and will.

Satan schemes, plots, and deceives (2 Corinthians 2:11; 1 Peter 5:8-9; Revelation 20:3). He was aware of Job's strengths (Job 1:6-12; 2:1-7) and Peter's weaknesses (Luke 22:31). He displays the emotions of pride (Isaiah 14:12-14; 1 Timothy 3:6) and wrath (Revelation 12:12). He can communicate with others (Zechariah 3:1-2), including Jesus (Luke 4:1-12), which supports the idea that he possesses personality. Throughout Scripture, personal pronouns are repeatedly used of Satan. The Bible makes it clear that Satan is a real person, the second-most powerful being in the universe, who is determined to do all he can to destroy and defeat God and His people.

4

Where did Satan come from? How did he fall?

Two principal passages of Scripture reveal Satan's origin and the beginning of the invisible war: Isaiah 14:12-19 and Ezekiel 28:11-19. These two texts describe his original condition in heaven, his sin, and his fall. They depict what we might call the Cosmic Skyfall. They chronicle Satan's creation, corruption, and condemnation.

Not everyone agrees that Satan is in view in these passages. However, if he is not, we are without any biblical record of his fall and rebellion against God. I believe that Satan is in fact the subject of these two passages and that we can piece the story of his fall together from what they tell us.

Ezekiel 28:11-19

Ezekiel 28:11-19 records the rise and fall of a person called the king of Tyre.

> Again the word of the LORD came to me saying, "Son of man, take up a lamentation over the king of Tyre and say to him, 'Thus says the Lord GOD,
>
> "You had the seal of perfection,
>   Full of wisdom and perfect in beauty.
> You were in Eden, the garden of God;
>   Every precious stone was your covering:
> The ruby, the topaz and the diamond;
> The beryl, the onyx and the jasper;
> The lapis lazuli, the turquoise and the emerald;
> And the gold, the workmanship of your settings
>   and sockets,
> Was in you.
>   On the day that you were created
> They were prepared.
> You were the anointed cherub who covers,
> And I placed you there.
> You were on the holy mountain of God;
> You walked in the midst of the stones of fire.
> You were blameless in your ways
> From the day you were created
> Until unrighteousness was found in you.
> By the abundance of your trade
> You were internally filled with violence,
> And you sinned;
> Therefore I have cast you as profane

From the mountain of God.
And I have destroyed you, O covering cherub,
From the midst of the stones of fire.
Your heart was lifted up because of your beauty;
You corrupted your wisdom by reason of your
   splendor.
I cast you to the ground;
I put you before kings,
That they may see you.
By the multitude of your iniquities,
In the unrighteousness of your trade
You profaned your sanctuaries.
Therefore I have brought fire from the midst of you;
It has consumed you,
And I have turned you to ashes on the earth
In the eyes of all who see you.
All who know you among the peoples
Are appalled at you;
You have become terrified
And you will cease to be forever.""'"

Ezekiel wrote these words in the sixth century BC during Judah's 70-year captivity in Babylon. Ezekiel's prophecies can be divided into three major sections.

Ezekiel 1–24	Judgment against Judah
Ezekiel 25–32	Judgment against Judah's neighbors
Ezekiel 33–48	Restoration of Judah and Israel

In the second of these three sections, Ezekiel deals with the coming judgment on Gentile nations surrounding Judah and predicts the fall of the leader of Tyre (28:2). Commentators generally agree that Ezekiel 28:2-10 refers to the Phoenician king Ethbaal III, who ruled over the seacoast stronghold of Tyre. He was an arrogant and greedy monarch, and Ezekiel prophesied the judgment that overtook him not long after this prophecy was written.

But Ezekiel 28:12 brings a sudden shift. The king of Tyre is suddenly introduced. He is not the same person as the leader of Tyre in verse 2. The leader in 28:2-10 is called a man twice (verses 2,9), while the king of Tyre is described in startling, supernatural language that goes far beyond what could be said of any human being. No person, especially the evil leader of Tyre, could be called perfect and blameless. Also, the king of Tyre was created (verses 13,15), which is a strange thing to say about a human king. Humans are born, not created. Based on these statements and descriptions, I believe this text describes Satan's prefallen state. By first describing the human leader of Tyre in verses 2-10 and then the king of Tyre in verses 12-19, Ezekiel appears to be revealing the supernatural power behind the human leader in the same way that Satan will be the energizing power behind the Antichrist in the end times (Revelation 13:2-4).[1]

If this understanding is correct, it tells us that before his fall, Satan enjoyed unparalleled privileges. He was the mightiest and most majestic of the angelic host. "The holy mountain of God" in verse 14 may refer to the very presence of God as Satan's abode before he fell. He enjoyed a coveted closeness to God Himself. He is also called the "anointed cherub" (verse 14) and the "covering cherub" (verse 16). Angels are divided into various classes, and the cherubim are a special class that are uniquely responsible to guard the presence and holiness of God.

The words "settings" and "sockets" in verse 13 can refer to tambourines and flutes, which gives support for the idea that Satan served as heavenly high priest who led all of heaven in divine worship. Verse 18 refers to his sanctuaries. It is impossible to be certain about the full meaning and implications of all these descriptions, but Donald Grey Barnhouse provides an explanation that brings these various parts together.

> The idea expressed in the word *covereth* has been widely interpreted by commentators…Here we begin to see him in his priestly function, associated with the cherubim who, even now, lead the worship of heaven (Revelation 4:9,10; 5:11-14), and who were near the throne of God…
>
> The fact that Lucifer had sanctuaries indicates both worship and priesthood. It would appear that he received the worship of the universe beneath him and offered it to the Creator above him…
>
> Here, in the presence of God, Lucifer brought the worship of a universe of creatures and received those commands from the Almighty, as the prophet of God, he transmitted to the worshiping creation. [2]

Before his fall, Satan was apparently the gatekeeper of God's glory, the heavenly high priest, the celestial worship leader. But the tragic turning point came in verse 15: "You were blameless in your ways from the day you were created, *until unrighteousness was found in you.*" This is the closest the Bible comes to pinpointing the origin of sin. Satan was perfect in all his attitudes and actions until the miserable moment when unrighteousness was found in him. Corruption was discovered in him. One moment it was not there, and the next moment, there it was. Satan was the first sinner in the universe.

The fall of Satan is described in verses 16-19, which begin, "By the abundance of your trade you were internally filled with violence, and you sinned." Arnold Fruchtenbaum describes what this means.

> That same figure was used of the human prince of Tyre in verses 1-10. For the prince of Tyre, this meant

going from port to port gathering wealth (v. 5). But for the king of Tyre, Satan, this meant going from angel to angel slandering God in order to win their allegiance…The words *they filled* refer to trafficking from angel to angel, bad-mouthing God. This led to violence, because it meant he led a revolt against God in Heaven.[3]

Satan embarked on a smear campaign, going from one angel to another, in an attempt to slander God. Referring to Satan's gamble to defeat God and take over heaven for himself, I once heard someone say, "Satan rolled the dice and came up snake eyes." Or as Erwin Lutzer notes, "His future was gambled in a slot machine that paid no dividends."[4]

Verse 17 reveals that the sin of Satan, the very first sin ever committed, was pride. "Your heart was lifted up because of your beauty; you corrupted your wisdom by reason of your splendor." Because of this sin, Satan was corrupted and cast down. His frightening fall was complete.

Isaiah 14:12-19

The second passage that I believe recounts Satan's original fall is Isaiah 14:12-19, which relates a similar story to the one found in Ezekiel.

> How you have fallen from heaven,
> O star of the morning, son of the dawn!
> You have been cut down to the earth,
> You who have weakened the nations!
> But you said in your heart,
> "I will ascend to heaven;
> I will raise my throne above the stars of God,
> And I will sit on the mount of assembly
> In the recesses of the north.
> I will ascend above the heights of the clouds;

I will make myself like the Most High."
Nevertheless you will be thrust down to Sheol,
To the recesses of the pit.
Those who see you will gaze at you,
They will ponder over you, saying,
"Is this the man who made the earth tremble,
Who shook kingdoms,
Who made the world like a wilderness
And overthrew its cities,
Who did not allow his prisoners to go home?"
All the kings of the nations lie in glory,
Each in his own tomb.
But you have been cast out of your tomb
Like a rejected branch,
Clothed with the slain who are pierced with a sword,
Who go down to the stones of the pit
Like a trampled corpse.

Commentators agree that Isaiah 14:4-11 describes the earthly, historic king of Babylon, yet as in Ezekiel 28, there is disagreement about whether the passage continues to describe the human leader or shifts to the ultimate power who energized him. I believe the "star of the morning" in verse 12 refers to Satan in his prefallen state. Verses 12-14 list his sins, and verses 15-19 describe his downfall.

Isaiah 14 parallels Ezekiel 28 in at least two ways. First, Satan is pictured in both texts as the ultimate power behind an evil human king. In Isaiah 14 he is the power behind the king of Babylon, and in Ezekiel 28 he operates as the force behind the prince of Tyre. Second, both passages identify pride as Satan's original sin. Isaiah 14:13-14 is often referred to as the five "I wills" of Satan. Inexplicably, he pitted his will against the will of God.

- "I will ascend to heaven." Satan wanted equality with his Creator.

- "I will raise my throne above the stars of God." The stars of God are other angels. Satan wanted to be above all creation and receive its worship.

- "I will sit on the mount of assembly in the recesses of the north." The mount of assembly is usually equated with the place where God rules. Satan wanted to occupy the zenith of authority.

- "I will ascend above the heights of the clouds." Clouds often symbolize the glory of God in Scripture. Satan wanted the glory due to God alone.

- "I will make myself like the Most High." Satan wanted to replace God.

In short, Satan's desire was to possess God's creation and be the sole authority over it. He tried to go up but was cast down.

Satan lost his place in heaven forever. As Erwin Lutzer notes: "No wonder Satan is furious. . . . Think of all that he had already given up. He could no longer be a prophet who could speak for God. He could no longer be a priest who would direct worship to God. He who wished to be like God has ended up the most unlike Him. In short, it was all loss and no gain."[5]

This is the opposite of what the Son of God did. He left the highest place in the universe at the right hand of God, humbled Himself, and came down all the way to the shame of the cross. As a result, God highly exalted Him (Philippians 2:5-11). For Jesus it was all gain and no loss. In God's economy the way up is down, and the way down is up. May this serve as an encouragement to us that God exalts the humble (James 4:10; 1 Peter 5:6).

To summarize what we have said so far about Satan's creation and corruption, here are seven key points.

1. Satan is a created being.

2. He was created perfect.

3. He held a high position, possibly the highest position under God.

4. He badmouthed God to the other angels to entice them to join him in a rebellion.

5. He sinned by becoming filled with pride.

6. He spearheaded a revolt against God in heaven.

7. He was cast down by God.

5

When did Satan become Satan? When did he fall?

Assuming that Isaiah 14 and Ezekiel 28 describe Satan's fall, we know that he was an unfallen angel and that he fell from that exalted position. But when did he fall? All agree that Satan fell at some point before Genesis 3, when he tempts Adam and Eve to disobey God. The question is, when before Genesis 3 did he fail and fall?

There are two main views on this issue.[1] Some believe that he fell before Genesis 1:1 and that God intended creation to be a staging ground to prove who has the right to rule. Others believe he fell at some point after God created the heavens and the earth but before Genesis 3, when he tempted Adam and Eve. That is, he fell sometime between Genesis 1:31 and 3:1.

It is impossible to be certain about this point, but some clues can help us piece the timing together. We begin with the fact that Satan was a created angel and that Job 38:7 tells us that when God created the universe, the angels rejoiced to see God's stunning handiwork. This means that the angels had been created prior to God's creation of the universe. It also indicates that at this time all the angels were still in an unfallen state and that all was harmonious as they joined together in rejoicing. Next, we know that God said everything was very good after the six days of creation (Genesis 1:31). Again, this indicates that all was still well in God's new universe, which seems incompatible with the existence of a host of fallen creatures.

So it seems best to place the fall of Satan and his host after the seventh day, when God rested and declared all things good in Genesis 1:31, but before Satan's appearance as the tempter in Genesis 3:1. Although it is impossible to be certain, it could be that after creation was completed and Satan saw its pristine state, including Adam and Eve and their perfect wonder and worship of God, he became jealous and coveted this worship for himself. As the gatekeeper of God's glory and the worship leader of heaven, he craved this worship for himself, sin was found in him, and the fall was final.

6

Why does God allow Satan and demons to exist?

According to Scripture, God created all things, including angels (Colossians 1:16). God is holy and sinless, so all angels were created holy and sinless as well. It is critical to remember that God did not create Satan or demons. God created a beautiful and anointed covering cherub and a host of perfect, unfallen angels. The anointed cherub led a rebellion against his Creator, resulting in his fall and the fall of one-third of the angelic host (Revelation 12:4). But the question still remains, why did God allow this to happen? God is omniscient, so He knew what would happen. And He is sovereign, so He could have prevented it from happening. Why didn't He?

This is one of the most difficult questions to answer, along with a similar question—why does God allow suffering and evil in the world? In some ways we can't fully answer these questions, yet in a broad sense we can know that in some way the presence of Satan and demons serves to glorify God, that is, to make Him known or put Him on display. God allows Satan to exist for sovereign reasons, many of which are undoubtedly known only to Himself. But we can rest in the fact that God is infinitely wise and infinitely loving and that He is working out His plan—the best plan to bring maximum glory to Himself.

7

How is Satan related to the serpent in the Garden of Eden?

Satan makes his entrance on the stage of human history in Genesis 3. He first appears as the tempter and deceiver of man.

> Now the serpent was more crafty than any beast of the field which the LORD God had made. And he said to the woman, "Indeed, has God said, 'You shall not eat from any tree of the garden'?" The woman said to the serpent, "From the fruit of the trees of the garden we may eat; but from the fruit of the tree which is in the middle of the garden, God has said, 'You shall not eat from it or touch it, or you will die.'" The serpent said to the woman, "You surely will not die! For God knows that in the day you eat from it your eyes will be opened, and you will be like God, knowing good and evil" (verses 1-6).

After the fall of Adam and Eve, God cursed each of the key players in the fall of man.

> The LORD God said to the serpent,
>> "Because you have done this,
>> Cursed are you more than all cattle,
>> And more than every beast of the field;
>> On your belly you will go,
>> And dust you will eat all the days of your life;
>> And I will put enmity between you and the woman,
>> And between your seed and her seed;
>> He shall bruise you on the head,
>> And you shall bruise him on the heel"
>>> (verses 14-15).

Genesis 3 does not mention the devil or call him by his name Satan, but the context and other passages of Scripture make clear that Satan was behind the activities of the serpent (Revelation 12:3,9). Genesis 3 refers to "the serpent" three times in the first six verses. This narrative raises many issues and questions, including the enduring difficulty of determining the relationship between Satan and the serpent. Is this all just symbolic and derived from pagan mythology? Did Satan transform himself into a serpent to disguise himself? Or did Satan indwell or inhabit an actual serpent?

I believe this passage is real history, not mythology. There is nothing in the text to alert the reader that this is mythological, and the New Testament takes the account of Adam and Eve and Satan in the Garden as historical (Matthew 19:4-6; John 8:44). The entire creation account is presented as a record of factual events that occurred. Other passages of Scripture refer to Satan embodying other creatures and working through them: the king of Babylon (Isaiah 14), the prince of Tyre (Ezekiel 28), and the final Antichrist (Revelation 13). We also know from Scripture that demons can inhabit human beings and take control of their bodies. With this in mind, we can posit that Satan chose the body of a serpent or snake as most suitable to disguise himself when he appeared to Eve to tempt her. Scripture later refers to Satan in various ways, including as a serpent and a dragon (2 Corinthians 11:3; Revelation 12:4,7,9,13).

Of course, the account of Satan indwelling a serpent to tempt Eve raises several other questions. What did the serpent originally look like before it was cursed? It was cursed to eat the dust of the ground and crawl on its belly—does that mean it was originally upright? And why didn't Eve think it was strange to hear a serpent talking? Could animals talk before the fall? The answers to these questions are beyond the scope of this book, but the comments of Henry Morris are interesting and helpful.

> There may really be no reason why we should not assume that, in the original creation, the serpent was a beautiful, upright animal with the ability to speak and converse with human beings. Such an interpretation would at least make the verses in the passage easier to understand, even though it may make them harder to believe...
>
> It is further possible that all these animals (other than the birds) were quadrupeds, except the serpent, who had the remarkable ability, with a strong vertebral skeleton supported by small limbs, to rear and hold itself erect when talking with Adam or Eve. After the temptation and fall, God altered the vocal equipment of the animals, including the structure of speech centers in their brains...The body of the serpent, in addition, was altered even further by eliminating his ability to stand erect, eye-to-eye with man as it were.
>
> Again it should be emphasized that the above interpretation is not intended dogmatically. The Bible is

not explicit on these matters and such explanations no doubt are hard to accept by the "modern mind." Nevertheless, they are not impossible or unreasonable in the context of the original creation and, indeed, appear to follow directly from the most natural and literal reading of the passage. [1]

Another related question is, why did God curse the serpent for something Satan did? Why was the serpent consigned to crawl on its belly for the actions of Satan? Certainty about this issue is impossible, but it could be that the lowly status of the serpent from that day forward was an object lesson for the rest of time. The curse on the snake was a picture or foreshadow of what will ultimately happen to Satan when he is subjugated by God. Through the curse on the serpent, God was saying to Satan, "You wanted to impersonate a snake? So be it! I will now change the character of the proud snake to a lowly animal, and in the same way you too will eventually be considered a lowly, subjugated creature, and the descendant of Eve will crush your head!" [2]

Whatever answers we may give to the specifics of this text, we can be sure that Satan is real, and that in his first temptation he used a disguise to make his seduction more palatable. He is still the master deceiver today. Deception is his calling card.

8

What are the different names and titles for Satan in the Bible?

Just as Jesus has many different titles that help us grasp His majesty, Satan has many names and titles in Scripture that unveil his wickedness. Some people have counted up to 28 different names and titles for the enemy of God and men. Here are 15 of the key ones.

Satan ("adversary" or "enemy") (Job 1:6-7; 1 Thessalonians 2:18)—This is the most common title for Satan in Scripture, occurring 18 times in the Old Testament and 34 times in the New Testament.

devil (*diabolos*, "slanderer" or "one who throws accusations") (1 Peter 5:8)—This is the second-most common name for our archenemy. It is found 36 times in the New Testament.

tempter (Matthew 4:3; 1 Thessalonians 3:5)

evil one (Matthew 13:38)

dragon (Revelation 12:3,9)

accuser (Revelation 12:10)

serpent (Genesis 3:1-4,14-15; Revelation 12:9)

father of lies (John 8:44)

star of the morning (Isaiah 14:12)

Beelzebub (Matthew 12:24)

ruler of the demons (Matthew 12:24)

Belial (2 Corinthians 6:15)

ruler of this world (John 12:31; 14:30)

god of this world (2 Corinthians 4:4)

prince of the power of the air (Ephesians 2:2)

9

Why is Satan called Lucifer?

The title Lucifer comes from Isaiah 14:12, which refers to Satan as the "shining one" or "star" (Hebrew, *heylel*). In the Vulgate, a Latin translation, the world *heylel* was translated as "lucifer," which means "morning star" or "light bringing." Later this word was adopted as a proper noun, a name for Satan. The name reinforces the notion that before his fall, Satan was the most beautiful of all God's creation. He was a shining one. We must remember that even now he can disguise himself as an angel of light to attract and seduce the unsuspecting and naive (2 Corinthians 11:14).

10

What does Beelzebub mean?

In Matthew 12:24 the Pharisees call Satan Beelzebub (sometimes written Beelzebul). The word is Greek and comes from the Hebrew *Baalzebul*, which means "lord of the flies" or "lord of the dwelling." It was a title given to one of the pagan gods of the Philistine city of Ekron who allegedly protected his worshippers from swarms of flies. Baalzebul derives from another Hebrew word that means "lord of the filth." Taken together these words "are suggestive of flies swarming over the trash heap outside the city of Jerusalem."[1] This is an apt description of our arch-adversary, who rules over a swarm of demons and whose ultimate destiny is the smoldering lake of fire.

11

What are Satan's main activities today?

There's a story about a farmer who was frustrated by thieves who were constantly stealing his watermelons. He finally came up with a brilliant plan to thwart the thieves. He poisoned one watermelon and then put a sign in his watermelon field that read, "Warning—one of these watermelons has been poisoned."

The next day the farmer went out and discovered that none of his melons had been stolen because the thieves didn't know which one was poisoned. He was satisfied that his idea had worked and that the problem was solved.

But two days later the farmer came out to his field to find that his sign had been altered. Someone had changed it to read, "*Two* of these watermelons have been poisoned." The farmer had to destroy his entire crop because he didn't know which other melon was poisoned.

That's often what it is like in dealing with the devil. When you come up with a plan, he seems to come up with something better. When you put up a sign, he changes the wording. Regardless of the strategy you devise, you just can't outwit the devil.[1] E.M. Bounds offers a helpful perspective.

> The Devil is a very busy character. He does a big business, a very ugly business, but he does it well, that is, as well as an ugly business can be done. He has lots of experience, big brains, a black heart, great force, tireless energy, and is of great influence and great character. All his immense resources are used for evil purposes.[2]

Whether we know it or not, "We are opposed by a living, intelligent, resourceful and cunning enemy who can outlive the oldest

Christian, outwork the busiest, outfight the strongest and outwit the wisest." [3]

Ephesians 6:11 refers to "the schemes of the devil." The Greek word translated "schemes" is *methodeias*. The word is plural, so we know that Satan employs many methods and schemes to undermine our lives and ministries.

> The devil's brain is prolific with plans. He has many ways of doing many things. Perhaps he has many ways of doing each thing. With him nothing is stereotyped. He never runs in ruts. Fruitful, diverse, and ever fresh is his way of doing things. Indirect, cunning, and graceful are his plans. He acts by trickery, and always by guile. [4]

Second Corinthians 2:10-11 also refers to Satan's schemes, but here the Greek word is *noema*, which means "thought" or "purpose." Satan is feverishly implementing his methods, plans, and purposes. The Bible is clear that Satan is engaged in a multitude of nefarious activities. He destroys, deceives, discourages, demoralizes, disheartens, and distorts. He counterfeits, masquerades, clouds with illusion, and sows seeds of doubt.

Satan's main method is to disguise sin to make it appealing and attractive. He makes sin look good and seduces us to believe we have the ability to control our sin and its consequences. Satan tries to sabotage our contentment in Christ and convince us that he can offer something better. He lures the unsuspecting with the promise of happiness, but he hides the price that must be paid. Erwin Lutzer poignantly describes this ploy.

> The best he can do is to break our fellowship with God; he wants us to become contaminated with sin so that God is obscured…If he cannot keep us from heaven, at least he can keep us from usefulness on earth.

> What he would really like to do is to prove that he can meet our deepest needs more successfully than God. If we follow him, his argument goes, we can have more potential, fulfillment, and happiness. He will do for us what God cannot. We do not have to humble ourselves to be blessed. There is no need for confession of sin, no need for submission to the Almighty. What we need is to be self-absorbed, self-motivated, and self-driven. This, the serpent hisses, is what life is really all about…
>
> What Satan fears most is Christians who have found God to be delightful. He has nothing that can compete. [5]

The only way to combat this action by our adversary is to delight ourselves in the Lord.

George Mueller, who is famous for constructing and operating orphanages in England, spent considerable time in prayer and Bible reading every morning. He believed that the first duty of every Christian is to content and satisfy his soul in God. Mueller relates how he spent time with the Lord every morning until his soul was "happy in God." [6] Our delight in the Lord short-circuits Satan's offer of fool's gold.

We could describe many more strategies of Satan, but here is a simple list.

> promotes false philosophies (Colossians 2:8)
>
> empowers false religions (1 Corinthians 10:20)
>
> energizes false ministers (2 Corinthians 11:14-15)
>
> manufactures false doctrine (1 Timothy 4:1)
>
> sows false disciples (Matthew 13:24-30)
>
> influences governments (Daniel 10:13; Revelation 16:13-16; 20:3)

deceives and blinds the lost (2 Corinthians 4:4; 2 Timothy 2:26)

incites persecution of believers (Revelation 2:10,13)

accuses God's people (Zechariah 3:1; Revelation 12:10)

hinders Christian service (1 Thessalonians 2:18)

promotes division and disharmony (2 Corinthians 2:10-11)

raises doubt (Genesis 3:1-5)

tempts to...

  sin (Genesis 3:1-6)

  anger (Ephesians 4:26-27)

  pride (1 Timothy 3:6)

  self-reliance (1 Chronicles 21:1)

  sexual immorality (1 Corinthians 7:5)

  lying (Acts 5:3)

  discouragement (1 Peter 5:6-10)

A similar list that describes some of Satan's schemes is also helpful.

He is a cunning deceiver (2 Corinthians 11:3).

He is the adversary (1 Peter 5:8).

He is the father of all lies (John 8:44).

He is the slanderer (Revelation 13:6).

He is the tempter (Matthew 4:3).

He is the thief who comes to kill and destroy (John 10:10).

He is the murderer (John 8:44).

He is the evil one (Matthew 13:19).

He blinds the minds of unbelievers (2 Corinthians 4:4).

He intoxicates and captures the lost (2 Timothy 2:26).

He masquerades as an angel of light (2 Corinthians 11:14).

He roams the earth looking for someone to devour (1 Peter 5:8).

He plots crafty schemes to trick believers (2 Corinthians 2:11).

Of course, Satan's greatest deception is to convince people that they don't need Jesus Christ as their Savior from sin. Don't be duped by the devil. Don't fall for this grand deception. Come to Christ and believe in Him if you've never done so.

12

If Jesus defeated Satan at the cross, why is he still active today?

The Bible is clear that Satan is a defeated foe. His head was crushed at the cross by the conquering King, our Lord Jesus Christ. The New Testament gives ample evidence of this fact: Romans 8:37; 2 Corinthians 2:14-16; Colossians 2:15; Revelation 3:21; 5:5; 12:11. But that raises the very practical question, why are spiritual battles still raging? Why is Satan still such a formidable foe if he has been vanquished?

John Stott, in his classic *The Cross of Christ*, helps us understand why we are still involved in conflict after the crushing victory of Christ over Satan. Stott opens by saying, "What the New

Testament affirms, in its own uninhibited way, is that at the cross Jesus disarmed and triumphed over the devil, and all the 'principalities and powers' at his command."[1] He then masterfully traces the conquest of Satan as unfolding in six stages.[2]

1. the conquest *predicted* in the Garden (Genesis 3:15)

2. the conquest *begun* in the earthly ministry of Jesus

3. the conquest *achieved* at the cross (Colossians 2:13-15; Hebrews 2:14)

4. the conquest *affirmed and announced* at the resurrection (Ephesians 1:20-23; 1 Peter 3:22)

5. the conquest *extended* as the church goes on its mission (Acts 26:18; Colossians 1:13; 1 Thessalonians 1:9)

6. the conquest *consummated* at the coming of Christ (Psalm 110:1; Philippians 2:9-11; Revelation 20:10)

According to Hebrews 2:14, Satan's power has been broken. He has been overthrown.

The death and resurrection of Christ was the crucial turning point in the war between Satan and God. David Jeremiah tells a story that beautifully illustrates this exciting truth.

> It is said of Napoleon Bonaparte that as he attempted to conquer all the kingdoms of the known world, he spread out a map on a table, pointed to a specific place, and said to his lieutenants, "Sirs, if it were not for that red spot, I could conquer the world." The spot to which he pointed was the British Isles—the very nation that met Napoleon at Waterloo in Belgium and defeated him in league with a group of allied nations.
>
> I have no doubt that when Satan talks with his minions about conquering the world, he says the same

thing about the red hilltop of Calvary where Christ's blood was spilled: "If it were not for that red spot, I could rule the world!" But that red spot is what makes all the difference in our spiritual battle. We do not have to live in fear of the devil. We need enter only the spiritual battle to which we have been called, aware of its reality and its subtlety, and armed with the truth that the ultimate victory against Satan has already been achieved.[3]

We live today in the interval between the achievement and announcement of victory at the cross and the empty tomb, and the actualization of the victory at the second coming.

Erwin Lutzer describes Satan's situation this way: "Today he is out on bail. He is allowed to roam until his final judgment. The sentence to the lake of fire has only been postponed. The verdict has already been read. We have seen the lightning. The thunder is on the way." The lightning happened at Calvary. The thunder will clap when Christ comes.[4]

Our mission today is to see that victory extended as lost men and women are brought into the light. As John Stott says, "So every Christian conversion involves a power encounter in which the devil is obliged to relax his hold on somebody's life and the superior power of Christ is demonstrated."[5] He continues:

> To borrow Jesus' own metaphor, now that the strong man has been disarmed and bound, the time is ripe for us to raid his palace and plunder his goods.
>
> It is not quite so simple as that, however. For though the devil has been defeated, he has not yet conceded defeat. Although he has been overthrown, he has not yet been eliminated. In fact he continues to wield great power. This is the reason for the tension we feel in both our theology and our experience...

The devil has been defeated and dethroned. Far from this bringing his activities to an end, however, the rage he feels in the knowledge of his approaching doom leads him to redouble them. [6]

Satan is a vanquished foe, but he isn't going down without a fight. He will continue to oppose God and His people until he is bound in the abyss for 1000 years and ultimately cast into the lake of fire.

13

Can Satan cause physical sickness and disease?

In several places Scripture is clear that Satan and his demons can afflict people with physical maladies. In what was probably the first book of the Bible written, Job was afflicted with a terrible disease by Satan.

> Satan answered the LORD and said, "Skin for skin! Yes, all that a man has he will give for his life. However, put forth Your hand now, and touch his bone and his flesh; he will curse You to Your face." So the LORD said to Satan, "Behold, he is in your power, only spare his life."
> Then Satan went out from the presence of the LORD and smote Job with sore boils from the sole of his foot to the crown of his head. And he took a potsherd to scrape himself while he was sitting among the ashes (Job 2:4-8).

Satan could afflict Job only with God's permission, and he was restrained from taking Job's life. Nevertheless, he had the power to afflict Job with a terrible, painful disease.

The Gospels contain other instances of demonic diseases.

- *Muteness.* "As they were going out, a mute, demon-possessed man was brought to Him. After the demon was cast out, the mute man spoke; and the crowds were amazed, and were saying, 'Nothing like this has ever been seen in Israel'" (Matthew 9:32-33).

- *Blindness and muteness.* "A demon-possessed man who was blind and mute was brought to Jesus, and He healed him, so that the mute man spoke and saw" (Matthew 12:22).

- *Deafness.* "When Jesus saw that a crowd was rapidly gathering, He rebuked the unclean spirit, saying to it, 'You deaf and mute spirit, I command you, come out of him and do not enter him again'" (Mark 9:25).

- *Physical deformity.* "And there was a woman who for eighteen years had had a sickness caused by a spirit; and she was bent double, and could not straighten up at all...'And this woman, a daughter of Abraham as she is, whom Satan has bound for eighteen long years, should she not have been released from this bond on the Sabbath day?'" (Luke 13:11,16).

During the coming time of tribulation, for a span of five months, demonic spirits will afflict unbelievers with painful, physical torment (Revelation 9:7-10).

Robert Dean and Thomas Ice add this important caveat to keep in mind concerning Satan and sickness.

Although disease might have some demonic source, however, Satan still must work in and through the biological laws that God created. These maladies are not mystical diseases that befuddle physicians and are cast away by magical incantations as in paganism. A disease caused by Satan would still have all the pathology of a disease that is brought on naturally; the same cure that worked on the latter would work on the former.[1]

Also, we need to always remember that Satan cannot act outside the sovereign will of God.

--- 14 ---

What was the apostle Paul's "thorn in the flesh" from Satan?

In 2 Corinthians 12:1-6 the apostle Paul relates a time 14 years earlier when he was caught up (raptured) to the third heaven, to Paradise, the very presence of God. He then goes on to state that because of this astounding revelation, God gave him a "thorn in the flesh, a messenger of Satan" to keep him from becoming prideful and arrogant. Second Corinthians 12 moves from the third heaven to the thorn in the flesh. What a contrast!

> Because of the surpassing greatness of the revelations, for this reason, to keep me from exalting myself, there was given me a thorn in the flesh, a messenger of Satan to torment me—to keep me from exalting myself! Concerning this I implored the Lord three times that it might leave me. And He has said to me, "My grace is sufficient for you, for power is perfected in weakness." Most gladly, therefore, I will rather boast about my weaknesses, so that the power of Christ may dwell in me (2 Corinthians 12:7-9).

The word "thorn" (Greek, *skolops*) is very graphic. It can refer to a small, sharp object, such as a thorn, or it can be used to describe a larger pointed object, such as a stake. This emphasizes the painful nature of whatever afflicted Paul. It was like a stake driven into his flesh. The Greek word translated "torment" literally means "to strike with the fist," which again highlights the severity of this affliction.

There are three principal views of the nature of this thorn in Paul's flesh. First, some believe that the thorn was a demonic spirit (a "messenger of Satan") assigned especially to Paul to torment him in various ways.

Second, others maintain that the thorn was the group of Paul's detractors at Corinth who were satanically inspired to seduce the Corinthians to rebel against him. This view fits well into the context of 2 Corinthians 10–13, where Paul is countering his rivals at Corinth who were challenging his apostolic authority and leading the Corinthian Christians astray. These false teachers and the havoc they were fomenting were certainly painful as a thorn in Paul's side.

I once heard a preacher say in jest that Paul had been married at one time and had a nagging wife who was his thorn in the flesh. (It's just a joke.) That would be a thorn, but I don't think that's what this is talking about.

The third more sensible view, and the one that I hold, is that this thorn was a physical affliction. The fact that this thorn was in Paul's flesh (his body) indicates to me that this was some type of physical ailment that was satanically caused. Galatians 4:13 supports the view that Paul suffered from some serious physical problem. Many have speculated that the problem could have been epilepsy or malaria. In Galatians 4:15 Paul commends the Galatians for their willingness to pluck out their eyes and give them to him. Later, in Galatians 6:11, he mentions the large letters he used in writing to them with his own hand. From these descriptions, some have surmised that Paul suffered from an eye condition that affected his sight.

Whatever the particular ailment was, Paul understood that

God allowed Satan to afflict him with this thorn for Paul's own good, to keep him from succumbing to pride. Both God and Satan are involved together. God used Satan to accomplish His greater purposes and to benefit Job and Peter, and here He does the same thing with Paul. God is sovereign even over our suffering.

15

Can Satan cause mental disorders?

We have seen that Scripture plainly shows that Satan can cause physical sickness, and this seems to include mental afflictions as well. How far he can go in plaguing people with mental disorders is uncertain, but clearly in the case of those who are possessed or indwelled by demonic spirits, mental and psychological abnormalities seem to follow. (Demon possession and its implications are discussed in questions 69–73.) The mental disorders induced by demons include such bizarre behavior as violence (Matthew 8:28), outbursts of abnormal strength (Mark 5:4), screaming (verse 5), self-mutilation (also verse 5), foaming at the mouth (Mark 9:20), nakedness (Luke 8:27), and grinding of the teeth (Mark 9:18). In Matthew 17:15-18, demonic spirits caused a man to totally lose control of himself.

> "Lord, have mercy on my son, for he is a lunatic and is very ill; for he often falls into the fire and often into the water. I brought him to Your disciples, and they could not cure him." And Jesus answered and said, "You unbelieving and perverted generation, how long shall I be with you? How long shall I put up with you? Bring him here to Me." And Jesus rebuked him, and the demon came out of him, and the boy was cured at once.

Of course, we must remember that these conditions are probably rarely caused by Satan or demons. We live in a fallen world, where both physical and psychological problems arise from natural as well as supernatural sources. But some mental maladies can be traced to demonic origin, and we should not be ignorant of this biblical teaching.

16

Can Satan perform real miracles?

Satan is a powerful spirit being—the most powerful being in the universe next to God. He possesses the power to perform supernatural feats, including real miracles. The miracles he performs aren't just clever tricks or slick counterfeits. He employs real, supernatural exploits to deceive people. There are several examples of this in Scripture.

In Exodus, the magicians of Pharaoh, who were satanic sorcerers, were able to counter the miracles of Moses up to a certain point. They turned their wooden staffs into snakes (although Aaron's snake ate their snakes), turned water to blood, and duplicated the miracle of the frog infestation. However, when Moses struck the ground with his staff and gnats (lice) covered the land, even the magicians themselves were forced to admit, "This is the finger of God" (Exodus 8:19).

During the future time of tribulation on earth just before the second coming of Christ, Satan will pull out all the stops in a final war of deception.

> Then that lawless one will be revealed whom the Lord
> will slay with the breath of His mouth and bring to an
> end by the appearance of His coming; that is, the one

whose coming is in accord with the activity of Satan, with all power and signs and false wonders, and with all the deception of wickedness for those who perish, because they did not receive the love of the truth so as to be saved (2 Thessalonians 2:8-10).

Revelation 13:11-15 records the final deception of Satan by means of miracle-working power displayed through his emissaries, the Antichrist and his false prophet.

Then I saw another beast coming up out of the earth; and he had two horns like a lamb and he spoke as a dragon. He exercises all the authority of the first beast in his presence. And he makes the earth and those who dwell in it to worship the first beast, whose fatal wound was healed. He performs great signs, so that he even makes fire come down out of heaven to the earth in the presence of men. And he deceives those who dwell on the earth because of the signs which it was given him to perform in the presence of the beast, telling those who dwell on the earth to make an image to the beast who had the wound of the sword and has come to life. And it was given to him to give breath to the image of the beast, so that the image of the beast would even speak and cause as many as do not worship the image of the beast to be killed.

Satan is a manipulative miracle worker. For this reason, we need to "test the spirits to see whether they are from God" (1 John 4:1). The presence of miracles is not necessarily a proof that something is from God. Jesus said that some miracle workers who appear before Him in the last day will be cast out of heaven.

Not everyone who says to Me, "Lord, Lord," will enter the kingdom of heaven, but he who does the will of My

Father who is in heaven will enter. Many will say to Me on that day, "Lord, Lord, did we not prophesy in Your name, and in Your name cast out demons, and in Your name perform many miracles?" And then I will declare to them, "I never knew you; depart from Me, you who practice lawlessness" (Matthew 7:21-23).

The proof of godliness is not our miracles, but our message and the manner of life we live, which bears out its reality in our heart.

17

Can Satan kill people?

Jesus said Satan was "a murderer from the beginning" (John 8:44). This probably refers to Cain's murder of his brother Abel. This savage sin was motivated by Satan (1 John 3:12). In Job, Satan stirred up a great storm that killed Job's ten children. Later, God told Satan that he could afflict Job with illness but that he couldn't take his life, which means he must have wanted to kill Job and would have been able to do so had God not restrained him. E.M. Bounds vividly describes the vicious assault against Job and his family.

> Without a note of warning, as an awful surprise and shock, at one fell and desolating blow, his family of ten children are dead, his princely fortune gone, and one dark hour has robbed him of family and possessions. Stripped naked by the fearful rapidity and depth of this losses, he becomes homeless, childless, and friendless...
> Satan plunged Job from a serene and cloudless, heavenly height down to a midnight, starless and stormy.[1]

Satan can snuff out the lives of people. He is a monstrous

murderer. But again we must remember that God has the final say, even over death.

> See now that I, I am He,
> And there is no god besides Me;
> It is I who put to death and give life.
> I have wounded and it is I who heal,
> And there is no one who can deliver from My hand
> (Deuteronomy 32:39).

> When I saw Him, I fell at His feet like a dead man. And He placed His right hand on me, saying, "Do not be afraid; I am the first and the last, and the living One; and I was dead, and behold, I am alive forevermore, and I have the keys of death and of Hades" (Revelation 1:17-18).

One of the hellish weapons in Satan's arsenal is murder, yet only under the sovereign, watchful eye of God. Jesus holds the keys of death, and Satan cannot wrest them out of His almighty hand.

18

Can Satan control the weather?

In recent years our world has suffered some of the most devastating storms in recorded history. Sometimes the sins of the people in the affected areas are blamed for these storms. But it's important to remember that we live in a fallen world that is groaning until the Lord comes. Violent weather outbreaks are part of the curse we live under, and they strike the just and the unjust. But Scripture is also clear that on some limited occasions, Satan can cause destructive storms. Job provides a clear illustration.

The LORD said to Satan, "Have you considered My servant Job? For there is no one like him on the earth, a blameless and upright man, fearing God and turning away from evil." Then Satan answered the LORD, "Does Job fear God for nothing? Have You not made a hedge about him and his house and all that he has, on every side? You have blessed the work of his hands, and his possessions have increased in the land. But put forth Your hand now and touch all that he has; he will surely curse You to Your face." Then the LORD said to Satan, "Behold, all that he has is in your power, only do not put forth your hand on him." So Satan departed from the presence of the LORD...

Another [messenger] also came [to Job] and said, "Your sons and your daughters were eating and drinking wine in their oldest brother's house, and behold, a great wind came from across the wilderness and struck the four corners of the house, and it fell on the young people and they died, and I alone have escaped to tell you" (Job 1:8-12,18-19).

It's clear from Job 1 that God allowed Satan to stir up the great storm or tornado that decimated Job's family. We see another possible example of Satan's control of weather in Mark 4:37-39.

And there arose a fierce gale of wind, and the waves were breaking over the boat so much that the boat was already filling up. Jesus Himself was in the stern, asleep on the cushion; and they woke Him and said to Him, "Teacher, do You not care that we are perishing?" And He got up and rebuked the wind and said to the sea, "Hush, be still." And the wind died down and it became perfectly calm.

Jesus rebuked the storm and spoke directly to the raging seas. This is reminiscent of His encounters with demonic powers. The word "hush" literally means "be silent," and "be still" means "be muzzled." The words Jesus used strongly imply that demonic influence was behind this storm. D. Edmond Hiebert notes, "The dramatic form of the command to inanimate objects may suggest that Jesus recognized demonic powers behind the raging elements. It is noteworthy that 'rebuked' and 'be still' were used in 1:25 with reference to an exorcism."[1] I believe that Satan whipped up this sudden storm in an attempt to destroy Christ or at least some of His disciples. But Jesus spoke a few simple words, and the winds went dead calm and the sea instantly became like glass. The simplicity and brevity of His command speak to His absolute control. Satan can stir up storms, but Jesus is the Sovereign of the storms.

19

Can Satan raise the dead?

The answer to this question is no. Satan does not possess the power to give life. Only the Creator can give life. However, there is a time in the future when God will give Satan the power to raise the Antichrist from the dead. Revelation 13:3-4 describes the fatal wound and healing of the Antichrist (the beast).

> I saw one of his heads as if it had been slain, and his fatal wound was healed. And the whole earth was amazed and followed after the beast; and they worshiped the dragon because he gave his authority to the beast; and they worshiped the beast, saying, "Who is like the beast, and who is able to wage war with him?"

There are three main views on the meaning of these words. Some believe that the death and resurrection here refers to the demise of the Roman Empire in AD 476 and its comeback in the end times. In other words, this is talking about the empire rising from the dead, not a man. The main problem with this view is the response to the beast's restoration. Would the revival of the Roman Empire really cause the entire world to be awestruck as is described in Revelation 13:3? This response would be much more likely if this refers to a man than an empire. A revival of the Roman Empire would hardly leave the world dumbstruck and cause everyone to follow it. But if a great world leader were assassinated with a fatal head wound and raised up a few days later, this response is understandable.

The second view is that the beast in Revelation is an individual who suffers a seemingly fatal wound but only appears to be dead. Those who hold this view believe that the restoration is a faked or counterfeit resurrection. Proponents of this view resist the idea that the beast could actually die and come back to life because Satan has no power to restore life.

All Christians agree that only God has the power to resurrect the dead. This is a given. However, God could temporarily give Satan this ability if He chose to. I believe that's what will happen during the future tribulation. God's permission for Satan to do this will be part of the great delusion God will send to those who reject Him (2 Thessalonians 2:9-12).

According to Revelation 13:15, the false prophet will "give breath to the image of the beast, so that the image of the beast would even speak." If Satan has the power to give life to a dead idol, then why is it not also possible for him (with God's permission) to resurrect a man from the dead?[1] Additionally, the Greek words used of Christ's death and resurrection in Revelation are also used for the Antichrist's death and resurrection (see Revelation 2:8; 5:6; 13:3,12). As Charles Ryrie notes, "If Christ died actually, then it appears that this ruler will also actually die. But his wound would be healed, which can only mean restoration to life."[2]

Based on the clear language of Revelation, I believe that the Antichrist will actually die and come back to life in a striking parody of the death and resurrection of Jesus Christ. This astonishing event will happen at the midpoint of the seven-year tribulation and will coincide with Satan being cast out of heaven and having but a short time (Revelation 12:12). Realizing that time is running out, Satan will desperately duplicate the resurrection of Christ (as God allows) and personally seize control of the Antichrist. This will be part of the delusion and deception that God will allow during that special season of time at the end of the age.

From that point on, having come back from perdition and being indwelled by Satan, the Antichrist will have the power to perform all kinds of signs, wonders, and miracles and will unleash his final great work of deception. J.B. Smith describes the impact this astonishing event will have on the world in the end times.

> Just as the early spread and the perpetuity of the Christian faith are grounded upon the resurrection of Christ, so the all but universal worship and homage accorded the beast in the last half of the tribulation period can only be accounted for by the resurrection of the fallen emperor of Rome. [3]

20

Is Satan omniscient—is he all-knowing?

Remember that Satan is a creature, and he is defined and limited by some features common to all creatures, so he doesn't know everything. Only God is all-knowing (Isaiah 46:9-10). However, Satan does know a great deal. We must not underestimate Satan—he knows more than we do. But we dare not overestimate him either by attributing divine attributes to him. Erwin Lutzer offers this clarification.

God would never create a being who was as great and beautiful as He Himself is. Any created being would of necessity fall short of the limitless perfections of the Almighty. Lucifer was therefore much less than God, but evidently he was the "best" the Almighty could do.[1]

21

Does Satan know people's thoughts? Can he read minds?

I do not believe Satan can read our minds. According to Scripture, only the members of the Trinity know the thoughts of all people (1 Kings 8:39; Matthew 9:1-4; John 2:24). Also, there are no examples in Scripture of Satan or demons reading anyone's mind or knowing their thoughts.

However, Satan and his demonic minions (who are assigned to various areas and maybe even individual believers) have lived for millennia and know human nature very well. We can be sure they study and observe our lives and know our tendencies. Just as we can sometimes know our spouse or our children so well that we can know what they are thinking, demons at times can certainly sense what we are thinking as they observe our actions.

Still, there is no biblical warrant for believing they can read our minds.

22

Can Satan plant thoughts in people's minds?

This question is closely related to the previous one, and I believe the answer is the same. If Satan cannot read our minds, then it seems to follow that he cannot plant thoughts in our minds. In Job 1–2, Satan is turned loose on Job to attack him on every front, short of taking his life. However, there is no mention of Satan planting thoughts or desires in Job's mind. His assaults are all external. This is an argument from silence, but if Satan had the power to plant thoughts in people's minds, surely he would have unleashed this attack on Job as part of the all-out assault allowed by God. The fact that he did not plant thoughts in Job's mind indicates to me that he does not have the prerogative to do so.

Two main passages are used to assert that Satan has the power to plant thoughts in the mind. The first is Matthew 16:23. In response to Peter's rebuke of Christ for speaking of His coming death at the hand of the Jewish leaders, Jesus said to Peter, "Get behind Me, Satan. You are a stumbling block to Me; for you are not setting your mind on God interests, but man's." I don't believe Jesus is saying that Satan planted thoughts into Peter's mind. Jesus is simply saying that what Peter expressed was in line with Satan's way of thinking and his desires. Peter was reflecting the purposes of the enemy.

Second, in Acts 5:3, Peter said to Ananias, "Why has Satan filled your heart to lie to the Holy Spirit?" The Greek word translated "filled" means "to control or influence." Satan influenced Ananias to sin against the Lord, but that does not mean he put evil thoughts in his mind. We don't know how Satan influenced Ananias, but it could easily have been through appealing to his pride or desire for recognition. Nothing in this text clearly indicates that Satan implanted thoughts in his mind.

The only exception I would add is in the case of those who are demon possessed. Satan does appear to plant evil, destructive thoughts in their minds. But other than that limited exception, I see no evidence in Scripture of his ability to plant thoughts in the minds of people.

23

Can Satan and demons make people sin?

I like the story of the little girl who was once disciplined by her mother for kicking her little brother in the shins and then pulling his hair. "Sally," said her mother, "why did you let the devil make you kick your brother and pull his hair?"

"The devil made me kick him," she said, "but pulling his hair was my idea!"[1]

We can all probably relate to that story. I would love to blame all or at least part of my sin on Satan, but I don't believe that Satan and demons can make anyone sin. They cannot force human beings to act. Many times we would like to pawn off full responsibility onto the devil, but James 1:13-15 gives us a more realistic picture.

> Let no one say when he is tempted, "I am being tempted by God"; for God cannot be tempted by evil, and He Himself does not tempt anyone. But each one is tempted when he is carried away and enticed by his own lust. Then when lust has conceived, it gives birth to sin; and when sin is accomplished, it brings forth death.

Satan is not mentioned anywhere in this chain of events. Of course, he is a master tempter, and he and his demons are sometimes behind temptation, but he is often absent even from the temptation itself, let alone the sin.

James tells us that human sin ultimately originates in the will and volition of people. The sinful human heart is the engine of sin. However, it is important to remember that Satan can strongly influence our thinking and our acting. Second Corinthians 11:3 says, "But I am afraid that, as the serpent deceived Eve by his craftiness, your minds will be led astray from the simplicity and purity of devotion to Christ." Satan and his henchmen cannot make us sin, but they deceive and seduce us, leading our minds astray.

There's a funny yet insightful story about a woman who bought a very expensive dress. When she brought it home and told her husband how much she had spent on it, he said, "Why in the world would you buy such an expensive dress? You know we can't afford it."

The woman replied, "But, honey, you don't understand—the devil made me do it! I tried it on, and the devil said to me, 'You look awesome in that dress, girlfriend. That's you all over…you've got to have that dress.'"

"Then why didn't you tell the devil, 'Get behind me, Satan'?" the husband asked.

His wife said, "I did—but when he got behind me, he told me I looked good there too." [2]

The devil and demons can tell us that something looks good, but they cannot make us do it.

24

Does Satan control and influence world leaders and nations?

Satan loves politics. He is the greatest politician of all time. He politicked in heaven and convinced a third of the angels to join his rebellious political party. Since then he has toiled strenuously to influence others to follow his wicked will.

When Satan's origin is unveiled, he is pictured as the king of Tyre in Ezekiel 28 and the king of Babylon in Isaiah 14. So it's clear from the outset that Satan influences world leaders. This same activity is evident in Daniel 10, where demonic spirits are called the "prince of the kingdom of Persia" and the "prince of Greece." These are demons whose function is to influence the leaders of these nations to do their bidding, especially the persecution of the Jewish people, who were ruled by the Persians at the time of Daniel's writing.

In Revelation 16:13-16, Satan sends out demonic spirits to entice the leaders of the world's nations to gather their armies at Armageddon in northern Israel for the final great military campaign of this age. Revelation 20:3 says that Satan is cast into the abyss for 1000 years after the return of Christ to earth "so that he should not deceive the nations any longer." This indicates that deceiving the nations must be one of his main goals during this present age.

Merrill Unger addresses the topic of Satan, demons, and human government.

> In every age of human history and in every phase of
> daily life demons have played a tremendous and very
> important role. In no realm is their activity more

significant than in the sphere of human government...
[Most people] can see only the human actors upon
the stage of history. Wicked rulers, ruthless dictators,
tyrants, oppressors, kings, governments, and presi-
dents are, to them, the real and only characters in the
great drama of life as it affects the political realm. They
have no idea at all of the unseen realm of evil personalities, energizing and motivating their human agents...

Human history is seen to be not merely an account
of human activities and events independent of spiritual
forces, but a continuous interaction of spiritual and
human personalities, in which demons play a prominent part.[1]

This means that when you see godless world leaders wreaking
havoc, spewing out threats, killing their own people, trampling
basic human rights, and fomenting anti-Semitism, remember that
even though they are ultimately responsible for their actions, an
evil force is at work behind and through them, trying to bring the
world under Satan's control.

25

Does Satan know the future?

God knows everything that will happen and how and when it will
happen. He even knows every contingency—what will or could
happen if certain events occur. For that reason, God can predict
the future with 100 percent accuracy (Isaiah 41:21-23; 42:8-9;
44:6-7). Satan, on the other hand, knows a great deal, but he can
only make informed guesses based on his own experience and
what he sees. That's why false prophets in the Old Testament, who
were influenced by Satan, got their predictions wrong. Only God

can predict the future infallibly. A true prophet of God is correct 100 percent of the time (Deuteronomy 18:22).

Satan's inability to know the future is best demonstrated by his own failure to know what would happen as a result of his own rebellion. He had the power to make his own choice, but he evidently had no knowledge of the consequences of his decision.

26

Is Satan omnipresent— is he everywhere at the same time?

Martin Luther warned, "Satan is as close as your own clothes."[1]

That sounds good, but it's actually not true. Satan is not God, so he can be only one place at a time. This is evidenced in Revelation 12:7-12—a scene from the future time of tribulation in which Satan is permanently banned from heaven. His domain at that time will be limited to earth, and even one place on earth at a time. This means that when he is in Japan, he cannot be in Washington, DC. When he is battling in New York, he cannot be disrupting a revival in India. Undoubtedly, as a spirit being, he can move quickly from place to place. He can surely cover a lot of ground, but he will never be omnipresent. He will never be able to fill the universe with his presence.

We often blame things that happen to us on Satan, but we must remember that Satan can only be one place at a time, so he can directly tempt, deceive, and oppress only one person at a time. As R.C. Sproul points out, this may give us some comfort, although we have to also remember that he has a host of demons who do his bidding throughout the earth.

I think we can take some solace in the thought that it's unlikely we'll ever meet with Satan in our lifetimes. He has bigger fish to fry. He's not going to chase after the little guys. But nevertheless, he has a host of minions, his demons, to do his work for him, and so they may surround us as close as our clothes, and satanic emissaries may besiege us, and we have to be alert to that. But it's unlikely that you and I will encounter the Prince of Darkness himself. I say that because he is not omnipresent. That is an attribute that belongs only to God. [2]

27

Is Satan omnipotent—is he as powerful as God?

It's been often noted that when people think about Satan, they tend toward extremes. Throughout church history, two serious distortions about the person and power of Satan have persisted. The first is to deny his reality or to fail to take him seriously as a potent spiritual adversary. The second distortion is to attribute greater power and authority to him than he actually possesses, as if God and Satan were equal combatants, fighting it out to the finish, vying for supremacy. Nothing could be further from the truth. The battle between God and Satan is no contest. God is all-powerful, or omnipotent; Satan is not. It's that clear-cut. Satan is a created being and is in no way equal to God. Not even close. This is proved by at least seven points.

1. Satan could not dethrone God in his rebellion. When he rebelled, God expelled him from His presence.

2. Apparently, all the angels, fallen and unfallen, regularly reported to God (Job 1:6; 2:1). This demonstrates God's authority over Satan and his angels.

3. God places clear limits and restraints on Satan in Job 1–2. Satan could not afflict Job without God's

permission, and God limited the extent of the suffering Satan could inflict upon him.

4. Satan could not successfully tempt Jesus into sinning (Matthew 4:1-11).

5. Satan will not be able to defeat God in the end (Revelation 19:11-21).

6. Satan will be bound for 1000 years in the abyss (Revelation 20:1-3).

7. Satan will be punished by God forever in the lake of fire (Revelation 20:10).

Robert Lightner says it well:

> Satan must never be viewed as God's equal, vying with God for control of the world. God and Satan are not similar to the good side and dark side of the "force" portrayed in Star Wars…God and Satan are not in a cosmic struggle to gain control of the world, for God alone is in control and sovereign. Satan is like a dog on his master's leash. He cannot do anything anywhere, anytime, to anybody, without God's permission. Yes, he is God's enemy and ours, but he is an enemy who must obey God even though he hates Him.[1]

Erwin Lutzer agrees.

> The devil is just as much God's servant in his rebellion as he was God's servant in the days of his sweet obedience. Even today, he cannot act without God's express permission; he can neither tempt, coerce, demonize, nor make so much as a single plan without the consent and approval of God.[2]

As Martin Luther famously said, "The devil is God's devil."

To summarize the limitations on Satan's power and influence, "He is powerful, but not omnipotent. He is smart but not omniscient. He can travel the universe, but he is not omnipresent."[3]

28

Should Christians be afraid of Satan?

When considering the subject of fear, we need to remember that not all fear is unhealthy. Some fear is good and some is bad. Good fear serves a healthy purpose. It's a protective mechanism. Fear is an appropriate reaction to a burning building or a growling dog. A healthy dose of fright can keep a child from running across a busy road. Healthy fear protects us. And every person needs one kind of fear—the fear of God, or reverential awe of Him.

The fear of God is the key to combating unhealthy fear. When we fear God, we don't fear other things. The person who fears God has no need to fear anything else. When Christ is great, our fears are not. As fear of God expands, fears about life and death diminish, including the fear of Satan.

Undoubtedly, Satan is a powerful spirit being. He is a ferocious foe. But believers are not to fear him. Fear of Satan is bad or wrong fear. In Matthew 10:28 Jesus said, "Do not fear those who kill the body but are unable to kill the soul; but rather fear Him who is able to destroy both soul and body in hell." Believers have not been given a spirit of fear (2 Timothy 1:7).

However, this does not give us license to swing to the other extreme by mocking, insulting, and making fun of the devil. This behavior is foolish and unbiblical (2 Peter 2:10; Jude 8-9). We are not to tremble at the devil, but neither are we to trivialize him. All of God's people would do well to remember the reassuring words of Martin Luther.

And though this world with devils filled,
Should threaten to undo us;
We will not fear, for God has willed
His truth to triumph through us.

29

How does Satan gain a foothold in a person's life?

Ephesians 4:26-27 gives us clues that demons can gain a foothold in our lives by our behavior. "Be angry, and yet do not sin; do not let the sun go down on your anger, and do not give the devil an opportunity." Unresolved anger is singled out as a sin that gives the devil an opportunity to derail and defeat us. Demons seize upon it to nurture bitterness and resentment, which wreak havoc in our souls.

However, we would be shortsighted to believe that anger is the only sin that demons exploit. We can safely assume they will leverage any attitude or activity, including homosexuality, pornography, greed, raw ambition, unforgiveness, and jealousy. Sin must be ruthlessly resisted because it renders us vulnerable and allows the enemy to get close enough to launch his fiery darts.

A Haitian pastor illustrated to his congregation the need for eliminating entry points to the enemy. He told about a man who wanted to sell his house for $2000. Another family badly wanted it but could not afford the full price. After some serious haggling, the owner agreed to sell the house for half the asking price with just one stipulation: He would retain ownership of one small nail just over the door.

After several years, the original owner decided he wanted the house back, but the new owners were unwilling to sell. So the first owner found the carcass of a dead dog and hung it from the single nail he still owned. Soon the house became uninhabitable, and the family was forced to sell the house to the owner of the nail.

Here's the Haitian pastor's conclusion: "If we leave the devil with even one small peg in our life, he will return to hang his rotting garbage on it, making it unfit for Christ's habitation." [1] The peg in our heart disappears when we resist sin and confess it when it occurs.

30

How is Satan related to the occult?

The word "occult" comes from the Latin *occultus*, from the verb *occulere*, which means to cover up or hide. It refers to things that are mysterious, hidden, dark, and concealed. It encompasses a broad spectrum of practices that allegedly surpass or transcend human knowledge. Practitioners of the occult harness secret powers to manipulate people or circumstances. [1]

Occult practices are broadly divided into three main categories: divination (foretelling the future), magic (sorcery), and spiritism (contacting spirits of deceased people). Satan is the author of all false religion, including occultism. In a sense, Satan's original appeal to Adam and Eve was an occult temptation to seek hidden information beyond what God had revealed.

The Bible soundly condemns every form of occult practice (Deuteronomy 18:9-14), which includes modern practices such as fortune-telling, Eastern meditation, reading palms and tarot cards, channeling, astral projection, astrology, Ouija boards, séances, crystal balls, or any other similar activities. Acts 16:16-18 and 19:11-20 link the occult to demonism.

C. Fred Dickason crystalizes Satan's relationship to the occult.

Not all occultism is genuinely satanic. Human greed and self-seeking account for much of it. Perhaps as much as 90 percent of all fortune-telling is faked by frauds and swindlers. Yet Satan stands ready to pounce upon his victims who exhibit interest in the occult, for it is his domain. [2]

Obviously, believers should never practice or even dabble in any form of occultism.

31

Are UFOs the work of Satan and demons?

My family and I have vacationed for many years in Ruidoso, New Mexico. On our way from Edmond, Oklahoma, to Ruidoso, we travel through Roswell, the UFO capital of the world. I have visited the UFO museums there and have even traveled with the landowner to the alleged July 1947 crash site near Roswell. While I was there, a group from Los Angeles was filming a documentary, and I spent some time talking with a man who was part of the original group to arrive at the crash site. The conversation was fascinating.

I have often wondered how to explain some of the strange things people have seen down through the centuries. Many others seem to share this interest. Popular culture is teeming with interest in UFOs and aliens. Movies constantly bombard us with the notion of extraterrestrials and alien visitors to earth.

At the outset, in any consideration of UFOs, the most important point is that the vast majority of UFO sightings are easily explained in terms of natural phenomena. About 95 percent of all reported UFOs end up being IFOs (identified flying objects). They turn out to be mistakenly identified planets (especially

Venus), stars, landing lights from distant airplanes, atmospheric gases, weather balloons, satellites, blimps or airships, abnormal lights, rocket launchings, and various other phenomena. Some are simply hallucinations. This means that when someone claims to see a UFO, the safest, simplest assumption is that there is a natural explanation. The vast majority can easily be dismissed as natural phenomena. So when we discuss the nature of UFOs, only about 5 percent are really at issue.

Some people believe the Bible references UFOs. The most commonly cited passages are the pillar of cloud and pillar of fire that accompanied the Israelites during the wilderness wanderings (Exodus 13:21-22; 14:19-20), the theophany in Ezekiel 1, and the Bethlehem star. Of course, none of these passages can be interpreted in any reasonable way as referring to UFOs.

Some Christians and many non-Christians believe that life exists on other planets. All agree that the Bible is silent on this subject. The most common argument for intelligent life on other planets is the vastness of space—why would God create so many galaxies if He didn't intend to populate them? The biblical answer is found in Psalm 19: God uses the universe to reveal His power and glory. Ron Rhodes provides this explanation.

> We might say that the whole universe is God's "kindergarten" to teach us the ABCs of the reality of God... This then is why God created so many stars and planets—not to inhabit them with multiple life-forms but to serve as a testimony to His power and glory. It is not necessary to argue that simply because many planets exist in the universe on which life *could* exist, life *does* therefore exist on those planets. [1]

No one can prove or disprove extraterrestrial life with absolute certainty, but I do not believe there is intelligent life on other planets.

About 5 percent of UFOs defy natural explanation and the laws of physics. They can...

1. move at a high speed without causing a sonic boom

2. turn at right angles or stop in midair at speeds up to 16,000 mph

3. adapt to human perception, appearing in the nineteenth century as flying sea ships or arrows

4. seemingly vanish into thin air

5. sometimes avoid detection by radar, photos, or other devices

6. seemingly change shape, size, or color at will

Of course, some enthusiasts suggest that the government has advanced spacecraft built on secretive technology. But this kind of conspiracy theory lacks evidence and gets us nowhere. You would think that at least one scientist or government defector would live to tell us about it![2]

Most UFO sightings are not an object or a craft. They are reports of massive, multicolored, intense, pulsating, hypnotic lights, often accompanied by strange sounds. In other words, UFOs don't always behave like material objects ought to behave. Many renowned researchers also note that UFOs do not appear to come from outer space, but appear suddenly, as if from another dimension. UFOs are not observed approaching from other planets, but materialize instantly, seemingly out of nowhere. For this reason, they are often classified as "interdimensional." A large number of well-respected UFO researchers (who are not Christians) maintain that UFOs and aliens are from parallel dimensions, not other planets. The UFOs simply slip in and out of sequence with our own dimension.

Based on my research, I conclude that there are no genuine UFOs, aliens, or extraterrestrials. The 5 percent or so of inexplicable manifestations are probably best explained as demonic forces passing themselves off as extraterrestrial beings in order to draw and distract people away from the true God.

This raises the question, why would demons materialize in this way? What do they have to gain? Certainty on this point is impossible, and focusing on extraterrestrials, life on other planets, and the lie that life on earth evolved from alien sources distracts many people and possibly even sets up the world for various forms of delusion in the end times. Belief in UFOs fills many people's spiritual hunger with alleged higher sources of knowledge and experience. All of this is consistent with Satan's portrayal in Scripture as a masquerading deceiver (2 Corinthians 11:14).

In short, Satan will do anything to distract people from their real spiritual need and God's answer to that need in Jesus Christ. Demonic materialization disguised as UFOs or extraterrestrials is likely just another of the tactics Satan employs to deceive, delude, frighten, confuse, and mislead people.

32

Can Satan and demons be saved?

The Bible is unambiguous that Satan and demons will not be redeemed. Revelation 20:10 says that their final destination is the lake of fire (see also Matthew 8:29; Mark 1:24). While recognizing this fact, however, some people wonder if Satan and demons could possibly be saved. Even though we know they won't repent, could they? Is there any opportunity for them to repent and be delivered? Hebrews 2:14-16 provides the biblical answer.

> Therefore, since the children share in flesh and blood, He Himself likewise also partook of the same, that through death He might render powerless him who had the power of death, that is, the devil, and might free those who through fear of death were subject to slavery all their lives. For assuredly He does not give help to angels, but He gives help to the descendant of Abraham.

This passage tells us that Jesus became flesh and blood. He became fully human. He became one of us to free us from the power of sin and Satan. He took on humanity and died as a substitute for sinners. The One died for the many. But Hebrews 2:16 is clear that Jesus gave no help to angels—He made no provision for their salvation.

This is saying that Jesus did not become an angel to die for angels. It's also important to remember that angels are not a race like humans. All humans descended from one man and one woman. When Adam fell, the entire race was plunged into sin (Romans 5:12). Angels, however, do not marry and procreate (Mark 12:25). Each angelic being is a special creation of God. Each angel made his own choice to join Satan's rebellion or remain true to God. They did not all fall when Satan fell.

Since human beings are a race, Jesus could become a man and die for all humans. He could not become an angel to die for all angels. There is no atoning sacrifice or provision for the sin of Satan and fallen angels, so there can be no forgiveness for their iniquity.

33

What does "delivered over to Satan" mean?

The church at Corinth was the most carnal, divided church that the apostle Paul addressed. The church was plagued by disorders, divisions, and difficulties. Sexual immorality was rampant. One of the more grievous issues the church faced was the sexual relationship between a member of the church and his father's wife. "It is actually reported that there is immorality among you, and immorality of such a kind as does not exist even among the Gentiles, that someone has his father's wife" (1 Corinthians 5:1). The woman was his stepmother, not his mother. Still, this was an incestuous relationship in God's eyes (Leviticus 18:7-8). Sadly, instead of mourning over this scandalous, unrepentant sin, the Corinthians arrogantly accepted and possibly even applauded it. Paul's response was strong and unwavering.

> For I, on my part, though absent in body but present in spirit, have already judged him who has so committed this, as though I were present. In the name of our Lord Jesus, when you are assembled, and I with you in spirit, with the power of our Lord Jesus, I have decided to deliver such a one to Satan for the destruction of his flesh, so that his spirit may be saved in the day of the Lord Jesus (1 Corinthians 5:3-5).

What does delivering this man to Satan entail? "It means putting the guilty one out of the church, thus stripping him of the protection of the fellowship. In verse 2, Paul plainly said the offender was to be removed from their midst. He was to be cut off from the community of God's children and the Lord's Table."[1] Delivering the unrepentant offender to Satan was in effect putting him out of the church and into the domain of the devil. The "destruction of his flesh" probably refers to physical illness and even death.

> In any case, Paul's instruction certainly differs from the practices of the modern spiritual warfare movement. Rather than delivering people from Satan, he said that the church sometimes has the responsibility of delivering a person to Satan! Now that's a form of "deliverance ministry" few people speak about today. [2]

The only other place in Scripture that mentions someone being delivered over to Satan is 1 Timothy 1:18-20.

> This command I entrust to you, Timothy, my son, in accordance with the prophecies previously made concerning you, that by them you fight the good fight, keeping faith and a good conscience, which some have rejected and suffered shipwreck in regard to their faith. Among these are Hymenaeus and Alexander, whom I have handed over to Satan, so that they will be taught not to blaspheme.

These two men were undoubtedly ringleaders of false teaching at the church in Ephesus. They were to be expelled from the church for a remedial purpose—"so that they will be taught not to blaspheme." The Greek word translated "taught" means to discipline with physical punishment (see 1 Corinthians 11:32). Homer Kent offers this explanation:

> Excommunication from the church [church discipline] places the offender back in the world which is Satan's domain. Hence to deliver unto Satan can be understood as removal back to the world…Such a removal from the church was corrective in its intent. If the false teachers were allowed to continue in their evil practices,

they would not only lead others astray, but would delude themselves into a false sense of spiritual security. But removal into Satan's realm would cause the offenders to face the issues. If they were truly saved, the buffeting of Satan would cause them to see their error and forsake their sin. [3]

These texts reveal the sobering truth that God actually uses Satan as an instrument to judge people in the church. God did the same thing with King Saul in the Old Testament. When Saul chose to follow his own way instead of the Lord, God gave a demon permission to torment and terrorize him (1 Samuel 16:14). Many wonder whether Saul was genuinely a believer, but 1 Samuel 28:19 indicates that when he died, he was going to be with the prophet Samuel, who was clearly a believer.

Also, Saul's condition was not demon possession, so he cannot be used as an example of a believer who was demon possessed. He was troubled and influenced by them but not indwelt or possessed. God turned him over to Satan as a judgment for his sins, and the demon influenced him to try to kill David out of jealousy. Clearly, God uses Satan at times to discipline professing Christians for their sin to bring them to their senses.

34

Why did Satan argue with Michael the archangel about the body of Moses?

The book of Jude, which some view as a kind of foyer or introduction to the book of Revelation, includes an interesting reference to a confrontation between Michael and Satan over the dead body of Moses. "But Michael the archangel, when he disputed with the devil and argued about the body of Moses, did not dare pronounce against him a railing judgment, but said, 'The Lord rebuke you!'" (Jude 9).

This reference in Jude quotes from a first-century book called *The Assumption of Moses*. A copy of this work was discovered in Italy and first published in 1861. The quoting of one small part of this book by Jude does not mean that Jude considered the entire book to be inspired and part of Scripture. Biblical writers sometimes quote extrabiblical texts to support a point, but this doesn't mean that the entire writing is inspired (see Titus 1:12). Jude 14 references another noncanonical book known as 1 Enoch.

The question remains, however, why did Satan want Moses' body? *The Assumption of Moses* states two reasons why Satan said the body should be given to him: because Moses had murdered an Egyptian, and because Satan is the king of death and has a right to all dead bodies.

Either of these explanations could be correct, but two other reasons have been cited by teachers and theologians.

1. Satan may have wanted the body to create some kind of shrine to Moses or sacred relic that he could use to lead the nation into idolatry. With the propensity of the nation to fall into idolatry, this certainly makes sense. This idea gains further credence from the fact that the Israelites later worshipped the serpent of brass that Moses made to stay the plague of the serpents (2 Kings 18:4).

2. Satan may have desired to prevent Moses from appearing with Elijah and Jesus on the Mount of Transfiguration (Matthew 17:1-8). The main problem with this view is that it assumes Satan knew about

Moses' future appearance on the mountain. This seems to give too much knowledge to Satan.

Certainty about the reason for the battle between Michael and Satan over Moses' body is not possible, but the incident serves as another reminder of Satan's power and willingness to use any angle to achieve his devious purposes.

35

What is the "synagogue of Satan" in Revelation 2:9?

Writing to the suffering church at Smyrna, Jesus said, "I know your tribulation and your poverty (but you are rich), and the blasphemy by those who say they are Jews and are not, but are a synagogue of Satan" (Revelation 2:9). Evidently, in the city of Smyrna in western Asia Minor (modern-day Turkey), the believers were being persecuted by a group of Jewish agitators. Jewish persecution of believers was common throughout New Testament times (Acts 13:50; 14:2,5,19; 17:5; 26:2; 1 Thessalonians 2:14-15).

These opponents of the church at Smyrna are identified as Jews physically and outwardly, but Jesus said they weren't true Jews inwardly—that is, they hadn't experienced a true circumcision of the heart through faith in Christ. Robert Thomas explains the phrase "synagogue of Satan" that Jesus applies to them.

> According to Jesus' own words, they are rather a synagogue of Satan. This is not a synagogue building, of course, but the people who gathered there. They assembled and planned their assault on the church, putting themselves at the disposal of the devil to carry out his will. They may have claimed to be the assembly of the

Lord…but in heaven's eyes these people were not true Jews, but emissaries of the prime adversary of God and His people, the devil or Satan.[1]

Like the Jews in John 8:31-44, these Jews in Smyrna claimed to be the descendants of Abraham but were actually children of the devil, doing his work of persecuting the church.

36

What is "Satan's throne" in Revelation 2:13?

In His letter to the church at Pergamum, Jesus said, "I know where you dwell, where Satan's throne is; and you hold fast My name, and did not deny My faith even in the days of Antipas, My witness, My faithful one, who was killed among you, where Satan dwells." Twice in this verse Jesus refers to Satan being in Pergamum. There are four main views of why Pergamum was called Satan's throne.

1. Pergamum was the seat of worship of Asclepius, a Greek god whose image involved a snake. A temple to Asclepius was located there. The tie between Asclepius and serpents would connect with Satan in the minds of the believers.

2. The great altar of Zeus, rising to a height of 40 feet, was located on the acropolis of Pergamum. It is a stunning sight. Zeus was the king of the gods, so this could have singled out Pergamum as "Satan's throne."

3. Pergamum was filled with temples and idols of many gods: Asclepius, Zeus, Athena, Dionysius, and Demeter. This city may have been the most outwardly pagan of those mentioned in Revelation 2–3.

4. Emperor worship was prominent in Pergamum. It was an official center of the imperial cult.

Any of these views is possible, and even a combination of them is probable, but if forced to take one view, I favor the second view. The presence of this impressive altar to Zeus and its prominence in the city made Pergamum a uniquely pagan place, as if Satan had set up his headquarters there.

37

Does Satan live in hell?

Cartoonists picture Satan with horns, a red suit, and a pitchfork. Another popular misconception is that he currently resides in hell. Satan's ultimate destiny is hell, or the lake of fire (Revelation 20:10), but he is currently the "god of this world" (2 Corinthians 4:4), the "prince of the power of the air" (Ephesians 2:2), who is prowling around "like a roaring lion, seeking someone to devour" (1 Peter 5:8). The devil and his demons restlessly roam the heavens and earth. According to Job 1–2, they even have some limited access to the third heaven, where Satan accuses believers before the throne of God as he did with Job (see also Revelation 12:10). Satan is destined for hell, but presently he is alive and well in the unseen spirit world and on planet earth.

38

Did Jesus go to hell for three days after His death to be tortured by Satan?

There have always been questions about where Jesus was and what He was doing between His death and resurrection. Obviously His body was in the tomb, but where was His spirit? The Apostles' Creed supports the notion that Jesus visited the underworld during this interval. This is often called the *descensus ad infernus* (the descent into the inferno).

> I believe in God the Father Almighty,
> Maker of heaven and earth:
> And in Jesus Christ His only Son our Lord,
> Who was conceived by the Holy Ghost,
> Born of the virgin Mary,
> Suffered under Pontius Pilate,
> Was crucified, dead, and buried:
> *He descended into hell*;
> The third day He arose again from the dead;
> He ascended into heaven,
> And sitteth on the right hand of God the Father
>   Almighty;
> From thence he shall come to judge the quick
>   and the dead.
> I believe in the Holy Ghost;
> The holy catholic church;
> The communion of saints;
> The forgiveness of sins;
> The resurrection of the body,
> And the life everlasting. Amen. (Italics added.)

The words "He descended into hell" are the most disputed.

This sentence was not in the earliest versions but was added in the third century.

One erroneous view about where Jesus went after His death and what happened to Him is that He went to hell to be tortured by Satan to pay the ransom for sinners. This is often called the ransom theory of the atonement. This theory, developed by Origen (AD 185–254) and held by Augustine, teaches that Satan held people captive as victor in war and that as a result he was owed a ransom. To settle the legal claim that the devil had won the human race, the ransom was paid to Satan by Christ by suffering at his hands in hell. This view is still quite popular today among many "word of faith" preachers, who take it to the extreme.

Five serious problems with this view render it biblically unacceptable.

1. Jesus made it clear just before He died on the cross that He was going to Paradise when He died (Luke 23:43). Paradise is the presence of God in heaven (see 2 Corinthians 12:4; Revelation 2:7). So we know that the Spirit of Jesus went to heaven when He died, not to hell.

2. Scripture does not imply that Satan has any legitimate claim on sinners. This view gives Satan far too high a role.

3. Satan is not the one who must be satisfied for sinners to be redeemed. Sin is against God, and He is the One whose justice, holiness, and wrath must be placated and appeased.

4. Scripture teaches that Christ's atonement was a sacrifice to God the Father. Ephesians 5:2 says, "Walk in love, just as Christ also loved you and gave Himself

up for us, an offering and a sacrifice to God, as a
fragrant aroma."

5. As Jesus was expiring on the cross and before He
discharged His spirit, He cried out triumphantly, "It
is finished." The work of salvation was finished by the
death of Christ. There was no need for Him to go to
hell to be dragged around by Satan to finish the work
of atonement.

I do believe that sometime during the interval between His
death and resurrection, Jesus did make a brief trip to the underworld to announce His victory to the demonic spirits there, but
we will address that in question 64.

39

Will the Antichrist be Satan incarnate?

The Antichrist is presented in Scripture as a complete parody or
counterfeit of the true Christ. He is Christ's alter ego. Could he
also be the product of a counterfeit virgin birth? That he will be the
son of Satan himself? That he will be Satan incarnate? Some stu-
dents of Bible prophecy contend that just as Christ was the product of a human mother and the Holy Spirit (the God-man), the
Antichrist will be the product of a human mother and Satan himself (the counterfeit god-man, or devil-man). This was the view of
Jerome in the fourth century AD. As the counterfeit son, he would
have a supernatural origin. He would literally be Satan's son. Hol-
lywood has latched onto this idea and popularized it in such movies as *Rosemary's Baby* (1968) and *The Omen* (1976). In *Rosemary's
Baby* a Roman Catholic couple (played by Mia Farrow and John

Cassavetes) make a deal with the devil. As a result, the wife eventually gives birth to Satan incarnate. The movie is dark and disturbing—is there any biblical basis for its view of the man of sin?

Biblical support for this notion is drawn primarily from Genesis 3:15, where the Lord cursed the serpent and said,

> I will put enmity
> Between you and the woman,
> And between your seed and her seed;
> He shall bruise you on the head,
> And you shall bruise him on the heel.

The offspring of the woman in this passage is clearly the coming Messiah or Deliverer, who would crush the head of the serpent once and for all. But notice the reference to "your offspring," or the offspring of Satan, who will be the arch-adversary of the woman's offspring. For those who hold to a supernatural origin for the Antichrist, Genesis 3:15 is seen as the first prophecy of the coming Messiah as well as the first prophecy of the Antichrist.

The supernatural origin of the Antichrist is certainly possible, but it seems better to view the Antichrist not as Satan's literal son but as a man who is totally controlled by Satan. The Antichrist is consistently presented in the Bible as a man. In 2 Thessalonians 2:9 we read about his person and work: "The one whose coming is in accord with the activity of Satan, with all power and signs and false wonders." The Antichrist is described as an evil man who is energized by the power of Satan to do his wicked work.

Revelation 13:4 says that the dragon (Satan) gives his power to the beast (the Antichrist). This verse teaches that the Antichrist is able to do what he can do not because he is Satan's offspring but because Satan energizes and empowers him as his chosen human instrument for world rule.

A man named Adso wrote a book in about AD 950 called *Letter on the Origin and Time of the Antichrist*. In this work he countered the view held by many in his day that the Antichrist will be born from a virgin and contended that he will be born from the union of a human father and mother. Nevertheless, Adso maintains, "He will be conceived wholly in sin, generated in sin, born in sin. The devil will enter the womb of his mother at the very instant of conception. He will be fostered by the power of the devil and protected in his mother's womb."

Adso's view is the predominant view in church history and seems to be the most consistent with the way the Antichrist is described in the Bible. Whether Satan enters the Antichrist at the moment of conception is debatable, but the main point remains— the Antichrist will be fully human yet totally possessed by Satan. The dragon will give the Antichrist "his power and his throne and great authority" (Revelation 13:2,4).

In Revelation 12, Satan is depicted as a great red dragon who is cast out of heaven as the result of a great cosmic war. The chapter ends by noting that "the dragon was enraged," and chapter 13 begins with these words: "And the dragon stood on the sand of the seashore. Then I saw a beast coming up out of the sea." The scene here is dramatic. Satan, the enraged dragon, is standing on the seashore, probably a reference to the Mediterranean Sea, calling forth the beast, or Antichrist, from the sea of the nations so that Satan can embody him and bring his program for world dominion into full swing. John Phillips sketches this graphic description of the Antichrist and his relationship to Satan.

> The world will go delirious with delight at his manifestation. He will be the seeming answer to all its needs. He will be filled with all the fullness of Satan. Handsome, with a charming, rakish, devil-may-care

personality, a genius, superbly at home in all the scientific disciplines, brave as a lion, and with an air of mystery about him to tease the imagination or to chill the blood as occasion may serve, a brilliant conversationalist in a score of tongues, a soul-captivating orator, he will be the idol of all mankind. [1]

In another place, Phillips writes this:

> The Antichrist will be an attractive and charismatic figure, a genius, a demon-controlled, devil-taught charmer of men. He will have answers to the horrendous problems of mankind. He will be all things to all men: a political statesman, a social lion, a financial wizard, an intellectual giant, a religious deceiver, a masterful orator, a gifted organizer. He will be Satan's masterpiece of deception, the world's false messiah. With boundless enthusiasm the masses will follow him and readily enthrone him in their hearts as the world's savior and god. [2]

With all the developments we are currently witnessing, many wonder if Satan's masterpiece could be alive today. Ed Hindson warns, "Someone ominous is looming on the horizon of human existence. He may still be in the shadows for the moment, but he could suddenly burst forth on the scene at any time."[3] Prophecy teacher Gary Frazier paints this chilling picture.

> Somewhere at this moment there may be a young man growing to maturity. He is in all likelihood a brooding, thoughtful young man. Inside his heart, however, there is hellish rage. It boils like a cauldron of molten lead. He hates God. He despises Jesus Christ. He detests the Church. In his mind there is taking shape the form of a dream of conquest. He will disingenuously present

himself as a friend of Christ and the Church. Yet…He will, once empowered, pour out hell itself onto this world. Can the world produce such a prodigy? Hitler was once a little boy. Stalin was a lad. Nero was a child. The tenderness of childhood will be shaped by the devil into the terror of the *antichrist*. [4]

Jesus may be coming very soon. Thank God we are looking for Christ, not Antichrist!

40

What is the "unholy trinity"?

The existence of the holy Trinity is the foundation of all things. God—the great three in one—exists, has always existed, and will always exist. God is Trinitarian—He is one in essence, or nature, yet He is three in person. One simple way it has often been stated is that God is one *what* and three *whos*. There is one eternal, infinite God, yet He exists as three coequal, coeternal persons—Father, Son, and Holy Spirit.

Satan is the master counterfeiter. In the end times, he will mimic the true Trinity with his own terrible trio. Revelation 13 presents two beasts who will rule the world in tandem and be totally intoxicated with Satan's influence. The first beast, who rises from the sea, is the political and military leader. He is the final Antichrist. The second beast, who comes from the earth, is the religious and commercial head. This second beast is also known as the false prophet (Revelation 16:13; 19:20; 20:10). Along with Satan, these two rulers form the unholy trinity of the end times. Satan is the false father (the antifather), the first beast is the counterfeit son (the Antichrist), and the false prophet is the phony spirit (the anti-spirit). Donald Grey Barnhouse offers this explanation.

> The devil is making his last and greatest effort, a furious effort, to gain power and establish his kingdom upon the earth. He knows nothing better than to imitate God. Since God has succeeded by means of an incarnation and then by means of the work of the Holy Spirit, the devil will work by means of an incarnation in Antichrist and by the unholy spirit. [1]

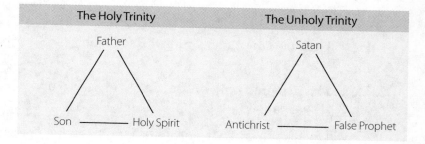

Just as the ministry of the Holy Spirit is to give glory to Christ and lead men to trust and worship Him, the chief ministry of the false prophet will be to glorify the Antichrist and lead people to trust and worship him. Here are five key ways the false prophet counterfeits the ministry of the Holy Spirit.

Holy Spirit	False Prophet
points men to Christ	points men to the Antichrist
instrument of divine revelation	instrument of satanic revelation
seals believers to God	marks unbelievers with the number of the Antichrist
builds the body of Christ	builds the empire of the Antichrist
enlightens men with the truth	deceives men by miracles

The false trinity will dominate the world for a brief stint, but they will share a common doom in the lake of fire (Revelation 20:10). They are no match for the great Three in One.

41

What will Satan do during the end times?

Satan will be very active during the end times, knowing that his time is short (Revelation 12:12). Here are ten of his main activities during the end times.

1. He will lead the false, unholy trinity (Revelation 13:2,11-12; 16:13).

2. He and his demonic army will be cast out of heaven by Michael (Revelation 12:7-9).

3. He will mercilessly persecute the Jewish people (Revelation 12:13-15).

4. He will know that his time is short, so he will pour out his wrath on the earth (Revelation 12:12).

5. He will accuse God's people before the throne (Revelation 12:10).

6. He will deceive the world (Revelation 12:9; 20:8,10).

7. He will gather the armies of the earth to Armageddon (Revelation 16:13-14).

8. He will be bound in the abyss for 1000 years (Revelation 20:3).

9. He will be released from the abyss and organize one final revolt against God (Revelation 20:7-10).

10. He will be cast into the lake of fire (Revelation 20:10).

42

Why is Satan bent on destroying the Jewish people?

In a conversation about religion, Fredrick II, King of Prussia (1740–1786), asked Joachim von Zieten, a cavalry general whom he esteemed highly as a Christian, for his plain and uncompromised views, "Give me proof for the truth of the Bible in two words!"

Zieten replied, "Your majesty, the Jews!"

General von Zieten's statement reflected not only his understanding of the miraculous preservation of the Jewish people, but also his belief that their preservation was for the purpose of bringing God's unfulfilled promises to pass. The continued existence of the Jewish people proved to him that God's Word was true because Scripture had promised that they would remain until all that had been prophesied concerning them was fulfilled. Remarkably, this expression of faith was made in a day when the land of Israel was desolate of a Jewish population and the majority of Jews were still scattered among the nations.[1]

The Jewish people have a long and storied history, having survived repeated persecution and pogroms. The Jews have been hunted and hounded for millennia wherever they have gone. Their struggles go far beyond anything that can be explained by purely natural causes. Something supernatural must lurk behind this agelong mistreatment of one particular group of people. The ultimate source of the opposition against Israel, according to Scripture, is not just prejudice—it's Satan. Revelation 12 pulls back the veil and shows us the real power behind all anti-Semitism. The Bible says that Satan is the archenemy of the Jewish people and of Jesus, their Messiah. In response to Satan's war on the Jewish people, God has appointed Michael the archangel as the protector of Israel. Some have called him the "guardian angel of Israel." In Daniel 12:1, Daniel is told, "Michael…stands guard over the sons of your people."

When God promised Abraham that the Messiah would come through his line, Satan began his mission to destroy Abraham's descendants, the Jewish people, to prevent the Messiah from coming. Satan instigated several unsuccessful attempts to eradicate the Jewish people.

- Pharaoh instigated a plan to kill the male Hebrew babies in Egypt.

- Haman tried to wipe out the Jews in the days of Esther (about 480 BC).

- The Syrian monarch Antiochus Epiphanes tried to destroy them in about 165 BC.

When Satan failed to prevent the Messiah from coming, he tried to kill Christ Himself. Satan tried to destroy Him right after His birth through the evil of King Herod (Matthew 2:13-16; Revelation 12:1-5). When this failed, he inspired the Jewish and Roman leaders to kill the Son of God. However, he failed to factor in the resurrection of Christ.

Satan couldn't prevent the Messiah from coming (plan A) or destroy Him (plan B), so he will continue trying to destroy the Jewish people, over whom the Messiah is to rule (plan C). Satan made his greatest attempt to destroy the Jewish people by means of the Third Reich. Adolph Hitler sent six million Jews to their deaths during his reign of terror. I once heard someone say that every time Satan tries to wipe out the Jews, they end up with a holiday. Pharaoh tried to destroy them, and the result was Passover. Haman tried in the days of Esther, and the Jews got the Feast of

Purim. Antiochus rose up against them, and the victorious Jews celebrated the Feast of Lights or Hanukkah. Hitler's diabolical plan finally resulted in the establishment of the modern state of Israel in May 1948.

American author and humorist Mark Twain highlighted the amazing survival of the Jews in *Harper's Magazine* in 1899.

> The Egyptian, the Babylonian, and the Persian rose, filled the planet with sound and splendor, then faded to dream-stuff and passed away; the Greek and the Roman followed, made a vast noise, and they are gone; other peoples have sprung up and held their torch high for a time, but it burned out, and they sit in twilight now, or have vanished. The Jew saw them all, beat them all, and is now what he always was, exhibiting no decadence, no infirmities of age, no weakening of his parts, no slowing of his energies, no dulling of his alert and aggressive mind. All things are mortal but the Jew; all other forces pass, but he remains. What is the secret of his immortality? [2]

Mark Twain was an agnostic and skeptic. He could recognize the miracle of Israel's preservation but could not understand the reason behind it.

But not only have the Jewish people survived as a distinct people down through the centuries, they have been restored to their ancient homeland against staggering odds. They have even revived their dead language. Since the founding of the modern state of Israel in 1948, Israel has been under constant harassment and frequent attack from the surrounding nations. The world community often takes the side of Israel's enemies even when Israel simply responds to unprovoked terror. Israel is under constant pressure to give up land for peace even though that strategy has never worked.

According to Scripture, Satan's war against Israel will continue in the end times. The Antichrist will begin his career by acting like the great friend of Israel, but in the great tribulation he will double-cross the Jews and slaughter them mercilessly (Daniel 7:25; 8:24; 11:44). The Antichrist will be empowered, controlled, and motivated by Satan, so his persecution of Israel must be an expression of Satan's hatred for Israel. Revelation 12 pictures Satan as a great red dragon and Israel as a woman whom the dragon pursues into the wilderness, where the woman is supernaturally protected by God for the final three and a half years of the tribulation. Satan is the ultimate anti-Semite. He hates the Jewish people because they are loved by God and because God has made special promises (covenants) with them that He will fulfill. Arthur Bloomfield describes Satan's plan to eradicate the Jews.

> Satan's attempt to destroy the Jews is of long standing. A number of times in history the Jews have narrowly escaped; in fact, the history of Israel is a history of narrow escapes…
>
> The history of the Jews is a history of expulsion from one country after another. When Satan gets the upper hand, the Jews are in trouble…
>
> God's whole future program revolves around Israel…
>
> God's entire kingdom program revolves around Israel. When Christ comes again, according to the prophet Zechariah, His feet shall stand upon the Mount of Olives that is before Jerusalem. The Jews will be the nucleus of the new kingdom. If Satan is to win this war and retain control of the earth, he must of necessity destroy all the Jews. That would prevent the establishing of the kingdom of God in the world. This is basic in the program of Satan. [3]

The primary tool Satan will use in the end times to carry out his extermination plan is his disciple and masterpiece—the Antichrist. He will be the last in a long line of persecutors who have tried to get rid of the Jews. But like all before him, he will fail because God will keep His promises to His people.

43

When will Satan and his angels be permanently expelled from heaven?

People are often surprised to learn that Satan and his demonic host presently have access to the third heaven, where God resides. This truth is taught in Job 1. When all the "sons of God" (angels) came to appear before God, Satan appeared there with them. Currently, Satan has some limited access to heaven. However, Scripture teaches that a time is coming when Satan and his angels will be permanently kicked out of heaven as the result of a cosmic battle with Michael the archangel and the host of unfallen angels who will fight with him (Revelation 12:7-9). Satan and his angels will be defeated in that battle, and from then on, they will be permanently denied access to heaven.

This cosmic war will occur at the midpoint of the seven-year tribulation because after being kicked out of heaven, Satan turns his wrath against the woman, who represents the believing remnant of Israel, and persecutes her for 1260 days (Revelation 12:6), or "a time and times and half a time" (verse 14), both of which are the final three and a half years of the tribulation. The beginning of the persecution of Israel also fits with Matthew 24:15, which marks the midpoint of the future tribulation.

When Satan is kicked out of heaven, he will be enraged because he will know that his time is short, only three and a half years. He will set out to inflict all the damage he can in the short time he has left. John Walvoord comments on this:

> From this point on in Revelation, therefore, Satan and his hosts are excluded from the third heaven, the presence of God, although their temporary dominion over the second heaven (outer space) and the first heaven (the sky) continues. Satan's defeat in heaven, however, is the occasion for him to be sent down to earth and explains the particular virulence of the great tribulation time. [1]

One of the factors that will make the great tribulation so terrible is the unmitigated wrath of Satan.

44

Why does Satan gather the armies of the world to Armageddon?

According to Scripture, a massive army will muster for the final battle of this age in an expansive valley in northern Israel that is overlooked by a small hill known as Armageddon (Mount Megiddo). These armies will be rallied to this place by demonic spirits under the direction of Satan.

> And I saw coming out of the mouth of the dragon and out of the mouth of the beast and out of the mouth of the false prophet, three unclean spirits like frogs; for they are spirits of demons, performing signs, which go out to the kings of the whole world, to gather them together for the war of the great day of God, the Almighty...And they gathered them together to the

place which in Hebrew is called Har-Magedon (Revelation 16:13-14,16).

The reason why Satan will influence these forces to gather there is not entirely clear. Scripture never clearly states why they assemble in the land of Israel. Some maintain that they will be assembled there from all over the world to challenge the Antichrist. After all, by the end of the tribulation and with all the judgments from God unleashed, the world will be in awful shape. Viewing the Antichrist as the source of the trouble, the nations may stage a global revolt to destroy him.

Others believe that the armies are gathered there in one final, all-out onslaught to eradicate the Jewish people. This campaign, energized by Satan, will be his last attempt to get rid of the Jews and thwart the promises of God. Of these two options the second one makes more sense to me because Revelation 16:13-16 indicates that the unclean spirits (demons) that gather the armies together will emanate from Satan, the Antichrist, and the false prophet. It seems unreasonable that Antichrist would want to gather the armies to destroy himself. Therefore, I believe the armies are drawn to Israel in a decisive anti-Semitic, satanic surge to rid the world of the Jewish people.

However, whatever the initial reason for the gathering of the armies, Scripture reveals that as the armies are gathered in Israel, they see the Lord Jesus coming from heaven and galvanize their efforts and animosity toward Him. "And I saw the beast and the kings of the earth and their armies assembled to make war against Him who sat on the horse and against His army" (Revelation 19:19). Their resistance, however, will be foolish and futile. One word from Jesus and it will all be over. He will slay them with the breath of His mouth (2 Thessalonians 2:8). Their defeat is certain before they even gather.

45

Does Satan really believe he can defeat God?

The Bible leaves no doubt that Satan will fail miserably in his attempt to defeat God. His doom is sure (Revelation 20:10). Does he really believe he has a chance of defeating God? Answering this question is difficult because the Bible never tells us what Satan believes about his own power in relation to God. Of course, Satan could be so deluded with pride that he actually believes he can ultimately outwit God and defeat Him in the end.

But it's also possible that he knows he's a defeated foe. He may recognize that his doom is sealed but refuse to go down without a fight. We can't know what's in his mind, but we can be sure that he will never succeed. He will finally be defeated by God and cast into the lake of fire.

46

When will Satan be bound in the abyss for 1000 years?

Revelation 19:11-21 describes the second coming of Jesus to earth and His victory over the forces gathered at Armageddon, including the Antichrist and the false prophet. Revelation 20:1-3 then describes the binding of Satan in the abyss for 1000 years.

There are two main views on the timing of this imprisonment of Satan. Some hold that this time of imprisonment is present. They believe that the 1000 years symbolize a long time and that it began when Jesus was on earth and bound Satan. Both amillennialists and postmillenialists hold this view. They maintain that the 1000-year reign of Christ is a spiritual kingdom that is present now and that Satan is currently bound so that he cannot deceive the nations. They often equate the binding of Satan in Revelation 20:1-3 with Matthew 12:29, Mark 3:27, and Colossians 2:15.

Premillennialists, on the other hand, who believe in a literal, future 1000-year reign of Christ on earth, believe that the incarceration of Satan is future. Three central points in the text and context of Revelation 20 support the futurist view of Satan's binding. The first is the flow of the context. The binding of Satan in the abyss for 1000 years follows immediately after the second coming of Christ in Revelation 19:11-21. The repeated phrase "And I saw" (32 times in the book of Revelation) moves the action along in a chronological sequence as John sees new visions (Revelation 19:11,19; 20:1,4,11; 21:1). The binding of Satan comes immediately after the return of Christ in this sequence of events. The natural reading of the text in its context favors the binding of Satan after the second coming of Christ. Nothing in the text signals the reader to leap back to Christ's first coming right after describing His second coming.

The second point in support of the future imprisonment of Satan is the consistency of this view with the way Satan is presented in the New Testament. Satan is portrayed as...

- the ruler of this world (John 12:31; 14:30)
- the god of this world (2 Corinthians 4:4)
- an angel of light (2 Corinthians 11:14)
- the prince of the power of the air (Ephesians 2:2)
- a roaring lion, seeking someone to devour (1 Peter 5:8)

The New Testament further states that Satan schemes against believers (2 Corinthians 2:11; Ephesians 6:11), hinders us (1 Thessalonians 2:18), accuses us (Revelation 12:10), and blinds the minds of the lost (2 Corinthians 4:4). This argues strongly against the notion that Satan is bound today. Amillennialists counter this by saying that Satan's power to deceive the nations is restricted today. Kim Riddlebarger, an amillennial scholar, explains this view.

> The amillennial interpretation of the binding of Satan is simply this. With the first advent of Jesus Christ and the coming of his kingdom, Satan was, in some sense, bound from the beginning of our Lord's messianic ministry…The binding of Satan simply means that Satan cannot deceive the nations until he is released at the end of the millennial age…
>
> The imagery that Satan is presently bound means that he cannot deceive God's people *en masse* nor can he attack the covenant community with relative impunity as he did before the coming of the Messiah. [1]

But Riddlebarger's claim is not supported by Scripture. He has to read into Revelation 20:1-3 the qualifications he makes.

Third, Satan is not bound today the way Revelation 20:1-3 describes. The binding of Satan is clearly set forth in Revelation 20:1-3 by a series of forceful actions.

> laid hold of
>
> bound
>
> threw him into the abyss
>
> shut it and sealed it over him

This description leaves little doubt that this binding of Satan is total during the 1000 years. "There is no indication that Satan has freedom to exercise any power during that period of time." [2] Since nothing like this happened at the first coming of Christ, this binding of Satan must be future.

47

Why will Satan be bound for 1000 years?

Revelation 20:3 tells us that Satan will be bound in the abyss for 1000 years "so that he would not deceive the nations any longer." Satan has spent thousands of years practicing his deception, but his days are numbered. He will be bound for the entire period of Christ's 1000-year reign while Jesus brings peace and prosperity to the planet. During this time he will be restrained from tempting people who are living on the earth.

48

Why will God release Satan from the abyss at the end of the 1000 years?

After being bound in the abyss for 1000 years while Jesus is ruling and reigning on the earth, Satan will be unchained and unleashed on the earth for one final stand—one last gasp—an event I call the "second coming of Satan." That much is clear, but the nagging question is, why? Why would God release Satan from the abyss at the end of the 1000 years? Why let him loose to unleash his rage on earth?

We don't know all the reasons why God will allow Satan a brief reprieve from his life sentence, but I believe that it will prove once and for all, beyond any doubt, that man's heart is black as midnight and that only the grace of God can save us. Revelation 20:7-10 says that when Satan is released, he will be able to gather a vast host of people on earth to rebel against the Lord. This will be the final rebellion.

A host of believers who live through the seven-year tribulation on earth will enter the 1000-year reign of Christ in their natural, mortal bodies. They will procreate during this time, and the earth will be repopulated. Everyone who enters the millennial kingdom will be a follower of Christ. However, many of their descendants will reject the Lord. According to Revelation 20:7-10, people who are born and raised during the millennium on earth, living under the righteous reign of the King of kings with Edenic conditions restored, will turn against the Lord the first time they get an opportunity.

> When the thousand years are completed, Satan will be released from his prison, and will come out to deceive the nations which are in the four corners of the earth, Gog and Magog, to gather them together for the war; the number of them is like the sand of the seashore. And they came up on the broad plain of the earth and surrounded the camp of the saints and the beloved city, and fire came down from heaven and devoured them. And the devil who deceived them was thrown into the lake of fire and brimstone, where the beast and the false prophet are also; and they will be tormented day and night forever and ever (Revelation 20:7-10).

This sounds unbelievable, but it's true. Man will quickly fall prey to the arch-deceiver. J. Vernon McGee provides valuable insight in answering why Satan will be released.

> When the late Dr. Chafer (founder of Dallas Theological Seminary) was once asked why God loosed Satan after he once had him bound, he replied, "If you will tell me why God let him loose in the first place, I will tell you why God lets him loose the second time." Apparently Satan is released at the end of the Millennium to

reveal that the ideal conditions of the kingdom under the personal reign of Christ do not change the human heart. This reveals the enormity of the enmity of man against God. Scripture is accurate when it describes the heart as "desperately wicked" and incurably so. Man is totally depraved. The loosing of Satan at the end of the 1,000 years proves it. [1]

Henry Morris makes a similar comment.

> One of the most amazing commentaries on the fallen human nature to be found in all the Word of God is right here in this passage. After one thousand years of a perfect environment, with an abundance of material possessions and spiritual instruction for everyone, no crime, no war, no external temptation to sin, with the personal presence of all the resurrected saints and even Christ Himself, and with Satan and all his demons bound in the abyss, there are still a multitude of unsaved men and women on earth who are ready to rebel against the Lord the first time they get a chance. [2]

When Satan is released for a brief time at the end of the millennium, his 1000-year prison sentence has not reformed his character. He has not changed. And mankind has not changed either. The second coming of Satan proves that Satan is still Satan and that man is still man even after 1000 years of the righteous, benevolent rule of Christ on earth. Even under the most ideal circumstances imaginable, man is still totally depraved and in desperate need of a new heart by the regeneration of the Spirit of God.

49

What finally happens to Satan?

Satan made his entrance on the stage of human history in Genesis 3 when he tempted Adam and Eve in the Garden of Eden. He will make his inglorious exit in Revelation 20:10 when he is finally cast into the lake of fire, where the Antichrist and the false prophet are confined. As the great reformer Martin Luther reminds us,

> The Prince of Darkness grim,
> We tremble not for him;
> His rage we can endure,
> For lo, his doom is sure;
> One little word shall fell him.

Part 2

Hell's Angels

What a vast and powerful array of aggressive, vicious, and cruel enemies. They are in heavenly places, the very place where Christ's power is located. These evil powers are over us, above us, and around us. They are too mighty for us. Against this invisible, innumerable, all-powerful, and vast array, we wrestle. Wrestling is a close conflict. It is intense and difficult conflict that tests all strength and strains every fiber. It is hand-to-hand, foot-to-foot, close contact. This conflict is not with men, though men may give us much opposition in our Christian course. Our chief trouble and our great war is not with man but with all the mighty evil forces of the Devil. It is a life-and-death struggle—a war for heaven and hell, for time and eternity.

E.M. Bounds

50

Do demons really exist?

Scripture refers to demons about 100 times, usually in the New Testament. Every New Testament author other than the author of Hebrews, although not every New Testament book, mentions demons or fallen angels. The authors of the New Testament believed in the reality of demons.

Jesus too taught that demons are real. He taught that Satan was the ruler of a host of demons (Matthew 12:22-28). He refers to Satan and "his angels" (Matthew 25:41; see also Revelation 12:9). Satan is real, so it follows that his angels are also real.

> A large portion of Christ's ministry involved the casting out of demons from those possessed...He gave His disciples power to cast out demons (Matthew 10:1) and viewed His victory over them as victory over Satan (Luke 10:17-18). He spoke of their reality and power to His disciples in private (Matthew 17:14-20). He never corrected anyone for believing in their existence and never gave any hint that they were not real. [1]

The authors of the New Testament and Jesus believed demons are real, and so should we.

51

What are demons?

Demons, like Satan, are personal beings, not nebulous, impersonal forces of evil. They possess all the characteristics of their master, Satan. Like Satan, they were created with intellect and will. They exercised that will and volition to throw in with Satan when he rebelled. C. Fred Dickason marshals strong evidence that demons are genuine spirit beings or persons.

1. *Personal pronouns.* The pronouns *I*, *me*, and *you* are applied to demons by Christ and by the demons themselves (Luke 8:27-30).

2. *Personal name.* Christ once asked a demon, "What is your name?" The answer came, "'Legion'; for many demons had entered him" (Luke 8:30).

3. *Speech.* Speech evidences personality in communication. The demons spoke to Christ, and Christ spoke to demons (Luke 4:33-35,41; 8:28-30).

4. *Intelligence.* Demons knew who the Lord Jesus was (Mark 1:23-24; Luke 4:34; 8:28). One gave a slave girl recognition of Paul and his ministry (Acts 16:16-17). The spirit also enabled her to determine secret information through fortune-telling, or divination.

5. *Emotions.* Demons evidence emotion in fear and trembling of judgment (Luke 8:28; James 2:19).

6. *Will.* Demons exercised will in appealing to Christ not to cast them into the abyss, but to allow them to enter swine (Luke 8:32). Christ's command to them is essentially a demand of His will over theirs, a demand they had to obey (Mark 1:27; Luke 4:35-36). [1]

E.M. Bounds summarizes the interaction of Jesus with demons, which proves their personality as real beings.

> Christ's encounters with those who were possessed by devils, or demons, illustrate His constant recognition of these fallen spirits as personal beings. He recognized their distinct individuality. He talked to them

and commanded them as persons. They knew Christ, confessed His divinity, bowed to His authority, and obeyed, however unwillingly, His commands. Jesus made a clear distinction between the human personality who was possessed by a demon, and the personality of the demon who held possession of the person. In his eyes, they were two distinct persons. [2]

All of these facts taken together demonstrate the personality of demons.

52

Where do they come from?

Interestingly, the Bible never explicitly reveals the origin of demonic spirits. For this reason, various suggestions have been offered. I will briefly mention the four main ones.

1. *They are the spirits of wicked, deceased humans.* This view is not consistent with Scripture because the Bible describes the spirits of the unsaved dead as confined in hades without any access to the earth (Luke 16:23).

2. *They are the disembodied spirits of a pre-Adamic race of people.* There is no evidence in Scripture that a pre-Adamic race existed, to say nothing about the quantum leap from such a race to demons. This is complete conjecture.

3. *They are the disembodied spirits of the monstrous offspring of the union described in Genesis 6:1-4.* Support for this view is drawn from the interpretation that the "sons of God" in Genesis 6 were demons who assumed physical

form and cohabited with women and that the result of these unions was monstrous offspring (*nephilim*), who perished in the flood. According to this view, the spirits of these mongrel beings became demons who are always seeking to inhabit bodies. Even if one holds that the "sons of God" were fallen angels, as I do, it does not follow that the spirits of their progeny are demonic spirits who are free to roam about the earth. This view is based on speculation, not Scripture.

4. *They are fallen angels who joined Satan in his original rebellion.* This is the best view for two main reasons. First, Satan is designated as the prince of demons (Matthew 12:24). If Satan is a fallen angel and the prince of demons, it makes sense that they are fallen angels too. Also, Matthew 25:41 refers to "the devil and his angels," and Revelation 12:7 mentions "the dragon and his angels." These texts indicate that demons are fallen angels.

   Second, according to Revelation 12:4, when the great dragon fell from heaven, his tail swept a third of the stars (symbolic of angels) to the earth with him. This reveals that the original satanic rebellion in heaven involved one-third of the heavenly host. These angels of Satan are now called demons.

Billy Graham gives this practical application from the fall of the Satan and his demons: "Today as always in the past, virtually no one can sin alone. The influences of sin are contagious."[1] Just as Satan did not sin alone, neither can we. Our sin affects others and can influence them to rebel against God.

53

How many demons are there?

All we know specifically about the number of demons is that they represent one-third of the original angelic host created by God (Revelation 12:4). Their number must be very large because during the tribulation, 200 million demons will be unleashed to pour out their fury and kill one-third of mankind (Revelation 9:16-19). This probably won't be the entire number of demons, so their number is at least in the hundreds of millions. At one point an entire legion of demons inhabited one man (Mark 5:9). A Roman legion was typically composed of 6000 soldiers. The number may not be intended to be exact, but it clearly indicates the man was infested with a hive of demonic spirits. This gives us some idea of the scope of the conflict around us and the number of nefarious forces we face.

We also know that the number of demons is fixed. Demons, like unfallen angels, don't marry and procreate to produce angelic offspring (Matthew 22:30). Therefore, whatever number of demons there were when they rebelled is the same number that exists today.

54

What are the names for demons in the Old Testament?

---

evil spirits (Judges 9:23; 1 Samuel 16:14-16; 18:10; 19:9)

immoral spirits (Hosea 4:12; 5:4)

prince of Persia, prince of Greece (Daniel 10:13,20)

destroying angels (Psalm 78:49)

lying spirits (1 Kings 22:22-23)

55

What are the names for demons in the New Testament?

demons (Matthew 8:31; 15:22; Mark 3:15; James 2:19)

unclean spirits (Matthew 10:1; Mark 1:23; Acts 5:16; Revelation 16:13)

the devil's angels (Matthew 25:41; Revelation 12:9)

rulers of darkness (Ephesians 6:12)

deceitful spirits (1 Timothy 4:1)

angels who did not keep their own domain (Jude 6)

locusts (Revelation 9:3)

horsemen (Revelation 9:16)

56

What are the main activities of demons?

The concept of asymmetric warfare has received lots of news coverage in recent years as a result of the war on terrorism. "Asymmetric" refers to something that is out of balance. In warfare it describes a situation in which the combatants are not equal.

Asymmetric warfare involves "the use of unconventional tactics to counter the overwhelming conventional military superiority of an adversary." When two forces are severely mismatched, the weaker force must use unusual methods of warfare in order to have any hope of prevailing in the conflict...

Today's asymmetric warfare comes in all varieties: hit-and-run attacks, suicide bombings, guerilla warfare, kidnapping, disinformation, and much more. Terrorists operate in small, loosely organized cells that spread across many nations. [1]

One military expert put it like this:

The ideal war is one that no one realizes is being waged, that is mostly invisible, not because its actions are camouflaged, but because they look like something else. War need never be declared again because we are always at war. [2]

You could hardly find a better statement to describe spiritual warfare and the activities of demons. Satan is the ultimate terrorist who led the first rebellion, the first insurgency in history, as he was lifted up in pride. Asymmetric warfare is a new name for a very old war—the invisible spiritual world war that's been raging through the ages. As we have seen, Satan is neither omnipresent, nor omnipotent, nor omniscient, but his evil influence is greatly enhanced by his hellish host, who are spread throughout the world as his global terror network. Moreover, since they are spirit beings, not limited to material bodies, they can no doubt move very quickly from one location to another.

Among their many activities, demons...

- may cause mental illness or physical diseases (1 Samuel 16:14; Matthew 9:33; 12:22; 17:15-18; Mark 5:4-5; Luke 8:27-29; 9:37-42)

- can influence people to perversity (Leviticus 18:6-30; Deuteronomy 18:9-14)

- promote idolatry (Leviticus 17:7; Deuteronomy 32:17; Psalm 106:36-38; 1 Corinthians 10:20; Revelation 9:20)

- possess animals (Mark 5:13)

- possess unbelievers (Matthew 9:32-33; 10:8; Mark 6:13)

- promote false religion and cults (1 Timothy 4:1; 1 John 4:4)

- deny biblical truth (1 Timothy 3:16–4:3)

- hinder answers to prayers (Daniel 10:12-20)

- incite jealousy and division (James 3:13-16)

- oppose marriages and families (Ephesians 6:12 follows the section on marriage and family) [3]

J. Dwight Pentecost reminds us of the persistence of demons in carrying out these deadly duties.

> They serve Satan faithfully, without interruption in their service. They don't punch in at eight and go home at four thirty with a half-hour off for lunch and two coffee breaks a day, so that there are times when you are free from their activity because they are off the job. As spirit beings, possessed with spiritual bodies, they are not limited by space or by time. They can give constant attendance to you wherever you are and whatever you are doing...They persist in executing the will of Satan

for you. And Satan's will for you is to defeat the will of God for you at any moment in your life. [4]

Understanding the activities of demons against us and their relentless attack, may we be stirred to vigilance and humble dependence on the Lord.

57

Are some demons worse than others?

The fact that some demons today are free to wander about (Ephesians 6:12) and some are bound indicates that some of them have gone too far and that God has removed them from circulation. When Jesus encountered the demoniac possessed by a legion of demons, the demons begged Jesus not to send them to the abyss but to allow them to enter a herd of pigs nearby (Luke 8:30-32). The demons' fear indicates that they believed they may have crossed a spiritual boundary that would result in their incarceration. Just as some people are less restrained than others in their sinful behavior, some demonic spirits are more evil than others and suffer consequences for it even now.

58

Are fallen angels referred to as "the sons of God" in Genesis 6?

Genesis 6:1-4 is one of the most enigmatic passages in Scripture.

> Now it came about, when men began to multiply on the face of the land, and daughters were born to them,

that the sons of God saw that the daughters of men were beautiful; and they took wives for themselves, whomever they chose. Then the LORD said, "My Spirit shall not strive with man forever, because he also is flesh; nevertheless his days shall be one hundred and twenty years." The Nephilim were on the earth in those days, and also afterward, when the sons of God came in to the daughters of men, and they bore children to them. Those were the mighty men who were of old, men of renown.

The interpretation of this passage turns on the identity of "the sons of God." Are they humans, or are they fallen angels (demons)? As you might suppose, there are several views.

The Line of Seth

Some view "the sons of God" as rebellious descendants of the godly line of Seth, and "the daughters of men" as ungodly descendants of Cain. Support for this view is based on the contrast in Genesis 4–5 between the two lines of descent from Adam—the Cainites and the Sethites. Augustine as well as the Reformers (Luther and Calvin) held this view. The problem with this interpretation is that not all the descendants of Seth were godly. Only one line of Seth was godly—the one that is traced in Genesis 5. If all the Sethites were a godly line, God would not have sent the flood. Also, if Moses wanted us to know that the sons of Seth married the daughters of Cain, why didn't he simply say so?

Tyrannical Despots

Another popular view is that "the sons of God" were power-hungry despots and tyrants who claimed deity for themselves, practiced polygamy, and perverted their mandate to rule the earth on God's behalf. The chief objection to this view is that there have always been evil despots on earth who seek power at any cost. Why is this particular sin singled out for mention, and how was it so severe as to trigger the global flood?

Demon-Possessed Tyrants

A third view is that "the sons of God" were demon-possessed tyrants. But that fails to explain the unique nature of the progeny. The children of these unions seem to be unique. They are called "nephilim" ("giants" in the KJV) and "mighty men." How would having a demon-possessed father explain the distinct nature of the offspring? Also, demon possession has always existed. Would the presence of demon possession demand the deluge?

Fallen Angels

I believe the natural reading of Genesis 6:1-4 supports a fourth interpretation—that during the days of Noah, a bizarre and abominable atrocity transpired, something so horrible, something so unthinkable, that it led to a tsunami of wickedness overflowing the earth. The corruption was so deep that no normal remedy would suffice. Only utter devastation could properly eradicate this infestation of wickedness.

The unprecedented sin was that "the sons of God" (fallen angelic beings) took on human form and cohabited with "the daughters of men" (human women). "The sons of God" were demons who had fallen in the original rebellion of Satan but now fell even further. Like an invading armada of extraterrestrial aliens, these fallen angels lusted after earthly women and left their proper abode, storming to earth to consummate their desire for strange flesh. I know this sounds odd, but let me make the case. Seven points support this interpretation of Genesis 6:1-4.

1. "Sons of God" (*bene elohim*) is found only three other times in the Old Testament. All three are found in the book of Job (1:6; 2:1;

38:7), and they all refer to angelic beings. A similar form is found in Daniel 3:25, which refers to either an angel or a theophany.

2. The Septuagint (a Greek translation of the Hebrew Old Testament) translates "sons of God" as "angels of God." This is significant because the Septuagint was translated in the third century BC and was the most commonly used version of the Old Testament during the apostolic period.

3. The angelic interpretation of Genesis 6:1-4 was the view of Judaism and the early church. The Jewish historian Flavius Josephus held the fallen-angel view of Genesis 6, as did Philo, Justin Martyr, Clement of Alexandria, Origen, Irenaeus, Cyprian, Tertullian, Ambrose, and Methodius. The second-century writing 1 Enoch 6–11 advocated the fallen-angel view of Genesis 6. Church history is never dispositive of any issue of biblical interpretation, but it should serve as a helpful guide.

4. Whatever is involved in Genesis 6, it must have been especially monstrous because it is the only specific case of evil mentioned immediately before the flood. It was so bad that it led to the destruction of the world and all but eight people. None of the other views do justice to the severity of judgment that follows.

5. There seems to be an intended contrast between the descriptions "sons of God" (angels) and "daughters of men" (human women), indicating that the "sons of God" are not human.

6. Three New Testament passages appear to refer to Genesis 6 and validate this view.

> Christ also died for sins once for all, the just for the unjust, so that He might bring us to God, having been put to death in the flesh, but made alive in the spirit; in which also He went and made proclamation to the spirits now in prison, who once were disobedient, when the patience of God kept waiting in the days of Noah, during the construction of the ark, in which a

few, that is, eight persons, were brought safely through
the water (1 Peter 3:18-20).

This passage is full of difficulties, but I believe it teaches that
Christ went to the underworld during the time between His death
and resurrection to proclaim His victory to the angels who sinned
in Genesis 6. For more about this, see question 64.

> For if God did not spare angels when they sinned, but
> cast them into hell and committed them to pits of
> darkness, reserved for judgment...(2 Peter 2:4).

In this text, the judgment of these angels is mentioned just
before the judgment of the world by the flood (verse 5). This fits
the chronology in Genesis.

> Angels who did not keep their own domain, but aban-
> doned their proper abode, He has kept in eternal bonds
> under darkness for the judgment of the great day, just
> as Sodom and Gomorrah and the cities around them,
> since they in the same way as these indulged in gross
> immorality and went after strange flesh, are exhibited
> as an example in undergoing the punishment of eter-
> nal fire (Jude 6-7).

These angels are bound, according to Jude, because they "abandoned their proper abode," "indulged in gross immorality," and
"went after strange flesh," as did the men of Sodom and Gomorrah. In other words, these angels went beyond their normal limitations and a forbidden sexual barrier God had appointed. This
too supports the fallen-angel view of Genesis 6.

7. The offspring of these unions were unique. They are
called "nephilim," which is from the Hebrew word *naphal* (to
fall upon). "Nephilim" is sometimes rendered "fallen ones." The
term "nephilim" is also found in Numbers 13:32-33 and is often

translated "giants." Based on Numbers 13:33, many believe that the nephilim were physical giants. This may be true, but the main connotation is their brutality and tyranny of falling upon others in violence. Concerning the offspring, John Phillips states, "They were probably the ancient Promethians, the prodigious creatures who gave to men the sins and secrets of the gods. The world had been a wicked place before; now it became wholly corrupt, and wickedness assumed enormous proportions."[1]

The children of these marriages are also called "mighty men [*gibborim*] who were of old, men of renown." This serves as a backdrop for ancient mythology that presents the gods coming down to cohabit with women. In ancient mythology the offspring of these unions were powerful beings, just as they are described in Genesis 6. James Boice makes this comment:

> What would be more natural than that this union would produce the "mighty men" of antiquity? Since this verse specifically refers to the "heroes of old," what would be more probable than that this is the origin of those stories of half-human, half-divine figures present in virtually all ancient mythologies? The stories of Homer and other writers would be embellished, of course, but they probably reflect memories of those ancient outstanding figures of the pre-flood period.[2]

Two problems with this fallen-angel interpretation of Genesis 6 are often cited. First, some simply complain that it seems too bizarre. It just raises too many questions. I agree that this interpretation is strange, even bizarre, but our task is to understand what the text says in its context and in conformity with the rest of Scripture, not to reject it because it seems too far-fetched. If the Bible says it occurred, we must accept it even if it isn't palatable. Many teachings of Scripture are difficult for us to fully understand and involve a degree of mystery.

The second objection is based on Matthew 22:30, which says, "In the resurrection they neither marry nor are given in marriage, but are like angels in heaven." All this passage says is that in heaven, humans, like angels, will not marry. However, we know that angels can take on human properties and look like men. They can walk, talk, breathe, and eat. Also, when they materialize, they are always masculine, and they are always referred to by masculine pronouns. Matthew 22:30 does not specifically preclude what is described in Genesis 6:1-4. It simply reinforces the notion that human beings in heaven will not marry.

Finally, why would demons do this? Why would demons take on human form and carry out this atrocity by intermarrying with women? I believe the reason for this action was to corrupt and pervert the human race. God had promised in Genesis 3:15 that the seed of the woman would crush the head of the serpent. Satan devised a plan to corrupt the entire human race by the intermarriage of demons and human beings. The Savior could not come from a corrupted lineage. So if Satan could succeed in corrupting the entire race, the promised Deliverer could not come. If Satan succeeded, all people would be lost.

That's why the flood was necessary—to preserve the human race intact, uncontaminated by Satan's scheme. By destroying the contaminated race and preserving uncontaminated Noah and his family, the way of redemption and the coming of the Redeemer was preserved. The flood was a cataclysmic judgment, but it was also an act of the matchless grace of God to make sure the plan of salvation stayed on track.

59

What are the different ranks in the demonic hierarchy?

Scripture reveals that angels are well organized. God is the Author of order and organization. Angels are ranked by class, including cherubim, seraphim, and living creatures. They also have numerous titles, including thrones, dominions, rulers (principalities), and authorities (Romans 8:38; Ephesians 1:21; 3:10; Colossians 1:16; 2:15). When these terms are listed together, they are usually consistent in sequence, which implies that the rank is in order of power.

Satan is the master mimic, so when he rebelled against God and formed his own kingdom, he patterned it after God's order of administration to maximize the effectiveness and influence of his forces. "With organization of information and cooperation in the ranks of the demons, their presence and power may be extremely efficient and effective." [1] Some of the same ranks are used for demons that are used for unfallen angels. Satan's armada is highly structured. It's like a well-organized army. Ephesians 6:12 pulls back the veil, allowing us to peer into the unseen world and into the invisible army of evil spiritual forces. "Our struggle is not against flesh and blood, but against the rulers, against the powers, against the world forces of this darkness, against the spiritual forces of wickedness in the heavenly places."

This describes a vast and highly organized hierarchy. John Stott refers to Ephesians 6:12 as a "full and frightening description of the forces arrayed against us." [2] They comprise what we might call the global satanic network, the spiritual mafia, the ultimate evil empire, or the cosmic potentates of this darkness. This world is in the grip of invisible cosmic rulers, an invisible world that's just as real as the visible world around us. Ephesians 6:12 uses these Greek words:

archai (principalities)

exousiai (powers)

kosmokratores (world rulers, forces of darkness)

pneumatika tes ponerias (spiritual forces of wickedness)

The first two terms overlap with the ranking of unfallen angels, but the last two are unique to demons. All these words are plural, indicating each category includes many beings under satanic leadership. Apparently these terms refer to various levels of authority and position. Satan's army has a defined, disciplined chain of command. The cosmic forces of darkness are "ordered and sub-ordered, coordinated and subordinated. They have the most perfect government—military in its discipline, absolute and orderly in its arrangement. They are under one supreme, dictatorial, powerful head, complete with rank and file and officers."[3]

Although it is impossible to understand the precise organizational hierarchy of the demonic world or the full meaning behind each of these various titles, the well-organized nature of Satan's army should grip the heart of every believer with the gravity of our battle and stir us to vigilance and dependence upon our great Commander in Chief for victory.

60

Are demons assigned to certain geographic areas?

Daniel 10 could be called the original *Angels and Demons*. It describes a scene of cosmic warfare between good angels and evil angels. In this gripping account, a good angel comes to comfort Daniel and convey a message to him. The angel delivers an answer to prayer and explains what was happening behind the *seen*.

> Then he said to me, "Do not be afraid, Daniel, for from the first day that you set your heart on understanding this and on humbling yourself before your God, your words were heard, and I have come in response to your words. But the prince of the kingdom of Persia was withstanding me for twenty-one days; then behold, Michael, one of the chief princes, came to help me, for I had been left there with the kings of Persia…"
>
> Then he said, "Do you understand why I came to you? But I shall now return to fight against the prince of Persia; so I am going forth, and behold, the prince of Greece is about to come. However, I will tell you what is inscribed in the writing of truth. Yet there is no one who stands firmly with me against these forces except Michael your prince" (Daniel 10:12-13,20-21).

The "prince of the kingdom of Persia" is a demon who was engaging in cosmic combat with the good angels who were trying to bring Daniel the answer to his prayer. Verse 20 mentions another demon, "the prince of Greece." The battle was so strenuous that Michael the archangel had to come help the angel in this conflict. The princes of Persia and Greece were demonic princes established over these respective nations. They were influencing these governments to oppose and hinder the nation of Israel, which was the topic of the visions Daniel received. In this sense, these demons were assigned, at least temporarily, to influence these particular nations and their leaders. This is part of the organized satanic hierarchy that encompasses the earth, as Donald Gray Barnhouse explains.

> The display of the forces of Satan, as recorded by Daniel, leads us to believe that the entire globe is organized under principalities, corresponding to earthly governments. If there is a Prince of Persia and a Prince of Greece, we may not be astonished if there is a Prince of Russia or a Prince of India, a Prince of Britain and a Prince of the United States. This is not mere conjecture for it is bluntly stated that earth government is in the hands of Satan…Satan may even have corporals in charge of municipal affairs. [1]

Although Satan's organization includes geographical areas, this is a far cry from the contemporary notion of "territorial spirits" that has been popularized in recent years. This topic of territorial spirits and cosmic-level spiritual warfare will be addressed further in question 87.

61

Can demons intercept our prayers and their answers?

Daniel 10 teaches us that God hears the prayers of His people immediately. As Daniel was praying to God, his words were being heard in heaven. Demons cannot keep our prayers from getting to heaven. But they can hinder the answers coming back to earth. Unseen spiritual warfare may delay answers to prayers. Daniel's answer was delayed for three weeks by demonic warfare.

Daniel 10 also reveals that forces of good and evil are all around us behind the flimsy facade of this world and that even holy, unfallen angels face opposition from demons.

62

Are there demons of lust, anger, alcoholism, and so on?

Many Christian leaders relate demons to various sinful attitudes, actions, or addictions, such as alcoholism, anger, lust, divorce, and the like. These evil spirits are viewed as the ultimate causes of the particular sins. Some point to 2 Timothy 1:7, which refers to a spirit of fear, as proof that there are evil spirits of various sins. However, the word "spirit" here refers to the attitude or disposition of fear, not a demonic spirit.

Of course, demons know our weaknesses and tempt us to sin, but to relate demons to specific sins, such as lust, anger, alcoholism, or drug addiction, is a simplistic view of the depravity of man and the sin problem. This unbiblical practice leads to frustration and failure. Overcoming sin is an ongoing, daily, lifelong issue, not a once-for-all act of rebuking a demon. The New Testament epistles never relate demonic spirits to specific sins or instruct believers to confront demons of particular sins. Rather, we are told to walk in the Spirit so we will not fulfill the desires of the flesh (Galatians 5:16). We are told to flee youthful lusts and pursue righteousness (2 Timothy 2:22). We are wise to follow God's method of dealing with the sin problem.

63

What are doctrines of demons?

One of the official documents distributed to Nazi guards overseeing the death camps of World War II included these words: "The camp's law is that those going to their death should be deceived until the end." [1] In the same way, Satan and his demons want to deceive people until the end. Their main method of deception is to disseminate false doctrine. First Timothy 4:1 reminds us, "The Spirit explicitly says that in later times some will fall away from the faith, paying attention to deceitful spirits and doctrines of demons." This verse draws a clear contrast between what the Holy Spirit is saying in the latter times and what deceitful spirits and demons are saying.

Satan is the mastermind of a campaign of mass deception. He knows that man is incurably religious—that men will bow the knee at some shrine. So he uses false religion and false teaching to keep people deceived until it's too late. You may have heard the illustration that one drop of cyanide in a jug of water is enough to kill you. The same is true with doctrine and teaching. Much of what is said can be truthful, yet one drop of serious error is enough to kill spiritually. Deceitful spirits are the instruments Satan uses to generate these false teachings. Doctrines of demons are the deadly ideas they produce. Years ago, I heard someone say, "The more truth an error contains, the more dangerous it is." Satan is glad to give people truth as long as he can squeeze in his drops of poison.

> False teaching will never enter your church with the name "Church of Satan" printed all over it. Deceitful spirits cleverly drape their doctrines in respectable, even pious robes of religion. The teaching appeals to the flesh and is presented with charm and charisma.

> False teachers speak convincingly to the issues of their
> day and often use the Scriptures (almost always out of
> context) to give the appearance of good-faith teaching.[2]

Demons worm these teachings into false religions, cults, pulpits, denominations, and seminary classrooms. Satan is mentioned in four of the seven letters to the churches in Revelation 2–3. We must never forget that "Satan is always at church before the preacher is in the pulpit or a member is in the pew. He comes to hinder the sower, to impoverish the soil, or to corrupt the seed."[3]

What are some of these demonic doctrines that are being peddled today? God is a myth. Creation happened by time and chance. Man is simply a higher form of animal. Man is inherently good. The Bible was written by men; it's not inspired by God. The Bible is filled with contradictions and errors. The Bible is one of many books that contain divine revelation. Man can get to heaven by his own good works. Jesus is not God, but a created being. Jesus did not physically rise from the dead. The miracles in the Bible never really happened. Everyone will go to heaven. There is no hell. God's highest goal is your happiness. God wants you rich and healthy.

Demons are lying spirits who want to destroy us body and soul and deceive us until the end. They are dead serious about this mission. We must be serious as well. We must know the truth and do all we can to spread it.

64

Did Jesus descend to the underworld after His death to make a proclamation to fallen angels?

One of the most interesting and difficult texts in the New Testament is 1 Peter 3:18-22.

> Christ also died for sins once for all, the just for the unjust, so that He might bring us to God, having been put to death in the flesh, but made alive in the spirit; in which also He went and made proclamation to the spirits now in prison, who once were disobedient, when the patience of God kept waiting in the days of Noah, during the construction of the ark, in which a few, that is, eight persons, were brought safely through the water. Corresponding to that, baptism now saves you—not the removal of dirt from the flesh, but an appeal to God for a good conscience—through the resurrection of Jesus Christ, who is at the right hand of God, having gone into heaven, after angels and authorities and powers had been subjected to Him.

The key statement is in verse 19, which says that Jesus went and made proclamation to the spirits now in prison. Three questions need to be answered to properly interpret this verse: When did Jesus make this proclamation, to whom did He make it, and what did He proclaim? There are three main interpretations of verse 19.

1. The preincarnate Christ preached to men through Noah in Noah's day. The people were disobedient, so they are now spirits in prison (hell). This was the view of Augustine and the Reformers.

2. Between His death and resurrection, Christ visited the

underworld and preached to human spirits in hell to give them a second chance for salvation. The problem with this view is that Jesus said those in hades have no second chance for salvation (Luke 16).

3. Between His death and resurrection, Christ visited the realm of imprisoned angels who sinned in Genesis 6. That is, He visited *tartarus* and proclaimed victory over the angels that are bound there.

The third view is the best view for five reasons.

1. This is the oldest view of this passage. It has antiquity on its side.

2. The chronological order supports this view. The text moves from Christ's death, to His proclamation to spirits in prison, to His resurrection, to His ascension and enthronement in heaven. The proclamation to the spirits in prison is between His death and resurrection.

3. It fits the account of Genesis 6:1-4 of sinning angels, which happened in the days of Noah.

4. Second Peter 2:4 and Jude 6-7 support the view that certain angels are bound today in *tartarus*. The word "spirits," when used by itself with no other qualifying statement, normally refers to angels.

5. First Peter 3:22 says Christ "is at the right hand of God, having gone into heaven, after angels and authorities and powers had been subjected to Him."

I believe that at some point between his death and resurrection, Jesus went to *tartarus* to announce to the angels who sinned in Genesis 6:1-4 His victory and their doom. This view is consistent with Colossians 2:14-15.

[God] canceled out the certificate of debt consisting of decrees against us, which was hostile to us; and He has taken it out of the way, having nailed it to the cross. When He had disarmed the rulers and authorities, He made a public display of them, having triumphed over them through Him.

The practical message of this passage is that Jesus is Lord of all. He is Lord of the lowest place (*tartarus*), Lord of the highest place (the right hand of God), and Lord of everything in between. That's our supreme comfort and confidence in the struggles of life.

65

Will the future tribulation include a massive demonic invasion of earth?

One of the strangest texts in Revelation is the description of a swarm of locust-like creatures rising out of the abyss in the end times.

> Then the fifth angel sounded, and I saw a star from heaven which had fallen to the earth; and the key of the bottomless pit was given to him. He opened the bottomless pit, and smoke went up out of the pit, like the smoke of a great furnace; and the sun and the air were darkened by the smoke of the pit. Then out of the smoke came locusts upon the earth, and power was given them, as the scorpions of the earth have power. They were told not to hurt the grass of the earth, nor any green thing, nor any tree, but only the men who do not have the seal of God on their foreheads. And they were not permitted to kill anyone, but to torment for five months; and their torment was like the torment

of a scorpion when it stings a man. And in those days men will seek death and will not find it; they will long to die, and death flees from them.

The appearance of the locusts was like horses prepared for battle; and on their heads appeared to be crowns like gold, and their faces were like the faces of men. They had hair like the hair of women, and their teeth were like the teeth of lions. They had breastplates like breastplates of iron; and the sound of their wings was like the sound of chariots, of many horses rushing to battle. They have tails like scorpions, and stings; and in their tails is their power to hurt men for five months. They have as king over them, the angel of the abyss; his name in Hebrew is Abaddon, and in the Greek he has the name Apollyon. The first woe is past; behold, two woes are still coming after these things (Revelation 9:1-12).

Several years ago I took my family to visit Carlsbad Caverns in New Mexico. I can still feel our slow descent into the bowels of the earth and smell the musty air of the caverns. The trip is an exciting adventure from start to finish. But the highlight of the trip is watching the nightly exodus of the bats from the cave at dusk when they feed on the insects in the surrounding area. As the thousands of bats fly out of the hole in the earth, the little light that remains at dusk is darkened by their flight. The scene is awesome in its beauty and uniqueness.

In a much more vivid and frightening scene, Revelation 9:2-3 describes the opening of the abyss, the release of the smoke of a great furnace, and myriads of locust-like beings swarming out on the entire earth and darkening the skies. Smoke billows forth from this prison of wickedness, and these locusts ooze from the abyss.

But what comes out of this subterranean pit to block the rays of the sun? What are these locusts that swarm out of the abyss and darken the skies of the earth? Are they literal locusts or some other creatures?

The locusts in Revelation 9 have been interpreted at different times in church history to symbolize heretics, the Goths, the Mohammedans, the mendicant orders, the Jesuits, the Protestants, the Saracens, and the Turks. However, the description in Revelation 9:2-5 reveals that these locusts are demonic beings in material, visible form. They are the uncanny denizens of the abyss, locusts of a hellish species animated with infernal powers. This passage describes an unbelievable demonic invasion of the earth by Satan's war corps in the last days.

These beings are generally like locusts, but they have eight other characteristics.

1. They are like horses.
2. They have crowns like gold on their heads.
3. They have faces like those of men.
4. They have long hair like that of women.
5. They have teeth like those of lions.
6. They have coverings like breastplates of iron.
7. They sound like chariots or horses going to battle.
8. They have tails like those of scorpions.

In each case the word "like" indicates that a comparison is being made and that something other than a literal description is intended. This doesn't mean these beings are not literal, but that John is describing them in the best way he can by comparing them to things that are familiar. Here's another way to list the descriptions of these locusts from hell.

heads—crowns like gold

faces—like men's

hair—like women's

teeth—like lion's

breastplates—like iron

wings—like the sound of chariots with many horses

tails—like scorpions

One of my friends read this description and said it sounded like a description of a rock star. Just think of the unbelievable appearance of these invaders from the abyss. They are long-haired, horse-shaped flying locusts with scorpion tails and golden crowns above human faces covered with skin like a coat of armor. They are infernal cherubim—a combination of the horse, the man, the woman, the lion, the scorpion, and the locust. Their size is not given, but they are clearly much larger than ordinary locusts.

Seven factors support the view that these beings are demons in material form.

1. Their leader is a fallen angel, or demon.

2. They come from the shaft of the abyss, which in the New Testament is consistently the place where some fallen angels or demons are consigned (Luke 8:31).

3. They cannot be literal locusts because their object of attack is people, not vegetation. Revelation 9:4 says, "They were told not to hurt the grass of the earth, nor any green thing, nor any tree, but only the men who do not have the seal of God on their foreheads." Literal locusts do just the opposite.

4. These locusts torture only those who do not belong to God. This is consistent with the activity of demons.

5. Demons can apparently appear in an assortment of material forms, both human and animal. In Revelation 16:13 demons appear as unclean frogs.

6. The description of these beings in Revelation 9:7-10 clearly goes far beyond anything from this world.

7. Literal locusts have no king over them. Proverbs 30:7 says, "The locusts have no king, yet go they forth all of them by bands." The locusts described in this passage have the "angel of the bottomless pit" as their leader (Revelation 9:11).

In the ancient world, nothing was more destructive than locusts. They were symbolic of destruction. The fifth trumpet judgment describes nothing less than the bowels of hell belching forth a horrid host of foul, fiendish demons to afflict unsaved people with excruciating pain and torture in the last days of the coming tribulation period.

Picture what the world would be like if the doors of the jails and penitentiaries of the earth were opened and the world's most vicious and violent criminals were set free, giving them full reign to practice their mayhem and infamies upon mankind. The scene in Revelation 9 is much, much worse. What will it be like when countless thousands of demons who have been chained in the abyss for thousands of years run rampant throughout the earth in visible form during this time of tribulation? It will be unspeakable!

Add to this the fact that in Revelation 12, Satan and his fallen host are cast down from heaven to the earth. The earth will be caught in the demonic crossfire as Satan and the fallen angels are cast from the atmospheric and divine heavens above down to the earth, and the demons from the abyss below are dredged up to the earth. The earth will literally be teeming with swarms of dreadful demonic beings. It will be an Auschwitz-like experience for those who must endure it. The diabolical forces from both heaven and hell will be unleashed to practice their unimaginable atrocities upon mankind. Revelation 9 reveals that in the last days, the earth will be invaded by a force of "aliens" unlike anything man could ever concoct in a special-effects lab.

66

Who is Abaddon, or Apollyon?

The leader of the demonic force in Revelation 9 is identified in verse 11. "They have as king over them, the angel of the abyss; his name in Hebrew is Abaddon, and in the Greek he has the name Apollyon." The words Abaddon and Apollyon mean "destruction" or "destroyer."

Many maintain that this is a reference to Satan, who leads the demonic army as its king. Certainly Satan is the king or leader of all the demons, but it doesn't necessarily mean that he is the direct leader of this special group of demons who arise from the abyss. Satan has no relation to the abyss until he is cast there in Revelation 20:1-3. In Revelation 9 he is still free to move about, so it seems strange at this point to identify him as the "angel of the abyss."

I hold that this is some other powerful fallen angel who is in charge of the abyss, where some fallen angels have been confined by God. Apollyon is an otherwise unknown fallen angel who is one of the leaders in Satan's organizational hierarchy.

67

Who are the four angels bound at the Euphrates River?

According to Revelation 9:13-15, four angels are bound at the Euphrates River.

> Then the sixth angel sounded, and I heard a voice from the four horns of the golden altar which is before God, one saying to the sixth angel who had the trumpet, "Release the four angels who are bound at the great river Euphrates." And the four angels, who had been prepared for the hour and day and month and year, were released, so that they would kill a third of mankind.

These are fallen angels or demons because unfallen angels are never spoken of as bound, while some fallen angels are bound (Jude 6). The particular demons are bound there for a specific period and purpose to serve as agents of God's wrath.

Why are these four evil angels bound at the Euphrates River? It's impossible to say for sure, but we do know that the Euphrates forms the northern boundary of the land promised to Abraham (Genesis 15:18) and that it will be dried up to prepare the way for the troops from the east to cross it for the final conflict at Armageddon (Revelation 16:12). Also, ancient Babylon, which was built on the Euphrates, will be rebuilt during the final tribulation (Revelation 17–18). Babylon is described in Revelation 18:2 as a hive of demonism. "And he cried out with a mighty voice, saying, 'Fallen, fallen is Babylon the great! She has become a dwelling place of demons and a prison of every unclean spirit, and a prison of every unclean and hateful bird.'" The demons at the Euphrates may have some connection to the swarming evil in this end-time city.

Whatever the special significance of the Euphrates in this context, Revelation 9:13-15 reveals God's total sovereignty. God will use these four demons to accomplish His purpose on His time schedule. God's will is accomplished in God's time.

68

Does the sixth trumpet judgment describe a human army of 200 million or a demonic one?

Almost 2000 years ago, the apostle John penned a prophecy that was unimaginable in that day.

> Then the sixth angel sounded, and I heard a voice from the four horns of the golden altar which is before God, one saying to the sixth angel who had the trumpet, "Release the four angels who are bound at the great river Euphrates." And the four angels, who had been prepared for the hour and day and month and year, were released, so that they would kill a third of mankind. The number of the armies of the horsemen was two hundred million; I heard the number of them (Revelation 9:13-16).

An army of 200 million! It's been estimated that this was probably about the entire population of the world in John's day. The Roman army in the first century was composed of 25 legions, or about 125,000 soldiers, with an auxiliary army of about the same size.[1] The end-times army mentioned in Revelation 9:16 is a thousand times that number.

The statement that it is prepared for "the hour and day and month and year so that they would kill a third of mankind" means simply that the four angels and the army they lead will be especially prepared for the day of battle that follows. This also indicates that God is the One who is in sovereign control over the army and the timing of its march.

Prophecy teachers have debated whether this refers to a literal, human army or a demonic cavalry that will be unleashed on the earth in the end times. Either view is possible.

A Human Army

Only in the past few decades has the assembling of a human army of this size been possible. As far as I know, the first person to point out the possible fulfillment of this prophecy in modern times was Dr. John Walvoord. His commentary on Revelation, published in 1966, mentioned in a footnote on Revelation 9:16 that China had the capability of fielding an army of 200,000,000.[2]

Those who hold the human-army view equate this army with the "kings from the East" who cross the dried-up Euphrates River (Revelation 16:12). These interpreters reason that both passages mention the Euphrates River as well as a large army. Some who adopt this view also see a reference to the army from the East in Daniel 11:45.

Demonic Armada

I believe it is better to view this colossal cavalry in Revelation 9 as an armada of demonic invaders that assaults the earth during the tribulation. I prefer this view for three key reasons.

1. The fifth trumpet judgment is clearly a demonic invasion of earth (demonic locusts), and the fifth and sixth trumpet judgments go together because they are the first two of three "woes." The linkage of these two trumpets supports interpreting the army released by the sixth trumpet as demonic.

2. This army is led by four fallen angels, just as the "locusts" of the fifth trumpet judgment were led by the fallen "angel of the abyss" (Revelation 9:14-15). Because the leaders are fallen angels, or demons, the troops they are leading are most likely demons.

3. Belching fire, brimstone, and smoke are always understood as supernatural weapons in the Bible and are connected with hell four times in Revelation (14:10-11; 19:20; 20:10; 21:8).

If this is in fact a demonic army in the end times, this means that during the tribulation period the earth will be overrun with demons who afflict men with great pain (the fifth trumpet, Revelation 9:10) and that this will be followed by another demonic outbreak that will ultimately slay one-third of the people on earth (the sixth trumpet, 9:15,18). But whether these 200 million horsemen are human or demonic, the prophecy is unparalleled, exacting the greatest death count in the history of the world.

69

What is demon possession?

When many people think of Satan, demons, and spiritual warfare, they immediately envision someone being controlled by demonic powers, or what is often called demon possession. This image may have come from movies or popular culture, but whatever the source, many people are curious about demon possession. Unfortunately, this curiosity is accompanied by deep confusion and controversy. The Bible never lays out a plain, systematic definition of demon possession, but there is enough evidence to establish a clear understanding of what is involved.

The Old Testament does not contain any clear cases of demon possession, so we are confined to the New Testament to understand this important topic. The New Testament employs two basic terms that inform our understanding of this subject. The first expression is either *echo* (to have) *daimonion* (demon) or *akatharton pneuma* (unclean spirit). Thus, it means to "have a demon" or to "have an unclean spirit" (Mark 3:30; Luke 7:33; John 7:20; Acts 8:7).

The second word is *daimonizomai* (to be demon possessed). It appears thirteen times in the New Testament, all of them in the Gospels (seven times in Matthew, four times in Mark, once in Luke, and once in John). These two expressions, "to have a demon" and "to be demon possessed" are synonymous because in Mark 5:15-16,18 the Gadarene demoniac is called "demon possessed," and in the parallel account in Luke 8:27 the same man is said to "have a demon" (literal translation). In the biblical accounts of demon possession, a demon takes up residence within a person's body. Alex Konya defines it as "the invasion of a victim's body by a demon (demons), in which the demon exercises living and sovereign control over the victim, which the victim cannot successfully resist."[1]

The notion of demon possession or control is reinforced by the terms that are used when a demon is expelled from a person. In the account of the Gerasene demoniac, Mark 5:13 says, "And coming out [of the man], the unclean spirits entered the swine." Luke 8:2 mentions Mary Magdalene, "from whom seven demons had gone out." In cases of demon possession, one or more demons indwell a person. Jesus gave His disciples an instructive illustration of demon possession in Matthew 12:43-45.

> Now when the unclean spirit goes out of a man, it passes through waterless places seeking rest, and does not find it. Then it says, "I will return to my house

from which I came"; and when it comes, it finds it unoccupied, swept, and put in order. Then it goes and takes along with it seven other spirits more wicked than itself, and they go in and live there; and the last state of that man becomes worse than the first. That is the way it will also be with this evil generation.

From this illustration we again see that demon possession involves demonic, unclean spirits living inside an individual.

> *Demonized* and *to have a demon* are used in Scripture of only one extreme type of demonic activity: to have one or more demons take up residence inside the body of a person and exercise control by overriding the individual's volition in relation to their bodily functions. The person's soul, his identity, is still there, although perhaps unconscious. His volition to believe or reject the gospel is still there, but his ability to control his body is not. These words never describe a case involving anything less, such as mere influence or putting ideas into someone's mind. For example, these terms never describe Satan's activities of accusation, temptation, deception, or persecution; they describe only the extreme case of being inwardly controlled by a demon.[2]

From the biblical evidence we can develop this concise definition: Demon possession is the direct, inward control by demons of their victim by their residing in him.[3]

70

Does demon possession still exist today?

Demon possession clearly existed in New Testament times. The New Testament does not specifically say that demons will continue to take up residence in people, but neither does it say they will not. For that reason, I believe demon possession continues today. Robert Lightner agrees.

> Since there is no scriptural teaching to the contrary we may assume that angels and demons continue to serve their respective masters. This would include bad angels, or demons, indwelling people. Since demons never possessed believers, we may be assured they do not do so now. Yet today demon possession of the unsaved may well occur occasionally.[1]

71

How can one tell the difference between mental illness and demon possession?

Schizophrenia and other serious mental disorders can resemble demon possession in several ways, such as altered personality, unusual physical strength, and altered voice. Treating a person suffering from schizophrenia or some other mental disorder as if he were demon possessed can have catastrophic effects. But treating the symptoms of a truly demon-possessed person as if he had a mental disorder is equally dangerous. Mental disorders are probably much more common than demon possession, but the possibility of demon possession in the case of an unbeliever should not be dismissed. How can we discern which condition a person has? Although there are no infallible guidelines on this issue, six helpful differences can aid in distinguishing between schizophrenia and demon possession.[1]

1. Schizophrenics sometimes speak incoherently but not with the refinement of a demon-possessed person.

2. A schizophrenic may believe he is someone he is not.

3. Schizophrenics often make outlandish, clairvoyant claims that are demonstrably false, but the extrasensory abilities of demon-possessed individuals are usually genuine.

4. Most schizophrenics don't react negatively to prayer or the name of Jesus, but demon-possessed people do.

5. Schizophrenics often respond to proper medication. Demon-possessed people do not.

6. The conditions of schizophrenia will continue after a person trusts Christ as Savior. The symptoms of demon possession will disappear as the Spirit takes up residence in the person and expels the demon.

Any Christian dealing with an unbeliever suspected of demon possession would be advised to seek out the help of a trusted Christian psychiatrist to aid in the proper diagnosis.

——— 72 ———

Can a believer in Christ be demon possessed?

I believe the Bible teaches that a Christian can be influenced, oppressed, and vexed by satanic and demonic powers, even acutely, but I do not believe that a Christian can be indwelled or possessed by a demonic spirit. In other words, a believer may be externally influenced by a demon, even severely, but not internally controlled or inhabited.

Many well-respected Christian theologians and Bible teachers disagree with me on this issue. Several passages in Scripture are often used to support their view:

> 1 Samuel 16:14 (King Saul)
>
> Matthew 16:23 (the apostle Peter)
>
> Luke 13:11-16 (a woman afflicted with a physical deformity)
>
> John 13:27 (Satan entering Judas)
>
> Acts 5:3 (Ananias)
>
> 1 Corinthians 5:5 (a man delivered over to Satan by Paul)
>
> 2 Corinthians 11:14 (Satan disguised as an angel of light)
>
> 2 Corinthians 12:7 (a messenger of Satan to buffet Paul)

But none of these passages actually say that a demon took up residence within a believer. Judas was clearly not a genuine believer (John 6:70). The "daughter of Abraham" in Luke 13 was simply a female citizen of Israel. The text does not say she was a believer in

Jesus. In each of these passages, one must read the idea of demon possession of a believer into the text rather than deriving it directly from the text. That is not a proper method of biblical interpretation. As John MacArthur notes, "In every instance when Christ and the apostles cast out demons, the demon-possessed people were unbelievers."[1]

Many people who maintain that believers can be demon possessed often base their conclusion on personal, subjective experience rather than God's Word.[2] They frequently cite accounts of what they or others have observed in the lives of professing Christians, and from these observations they conclude that believers in Christ can be demon possessed.

Of course, our experiences are not unimportant. They often validate the truth of Scripture. Paul used the experience of the Galatians to confirm their reception of the Holy Spirit by faith rather than works (Galatians 3:1-5). However, a correct interpretation of our experience will never contradict the clear teaching of Scripture. Every explanation of our experience must be carefully weighed against the truth of Scripture, and if it comes up short, it must be rejected. As with other issues, our final guide and authority must be God's Word, not our subjective understanding of human experience. With this important guideline in mind, here are three simple, biblical points that lead me to the conclusion that no believer can be inhabited by an evil spirit.

Spirit Indwelling

First, the Holy Spirit, the third member of the triune Godhead, dwells in every believer in Christ. First Corinthians 6:19 says, "Do you not know that your body is a temple of the Holy Spirit who is in you, whom you have from God, and that you are not your own?" The Holy Spirit inhabits all believers in Christ in this present age. He has converted their physical bodies into temples or dwelling places of God. It is unthinkable that the Holy Spirit would share His dwelling place with a foul spirit.

> What harmony has Christ with Belial, or what has a believer in common with an unbeliever? Or what agreement has the temple of God with idols? For we are the temple of the living God; just as God said, I will dwell in them and walk among them; and I will be their God, and they shall be My people (2 Corinthians 6:15-16).

First John 4:4 adds, "You are from God, little children, and have overcome them; because greater is He who is in you than he who is in the world." If the Spirit lives in a Christian, and the Spirit is greater than Satan or any demon, how could that demon ever enter the person and take up residence? Robert Dean and Thomas Ice make the same conclusion.

> A demon is not able to enter into and take control of a believer's physical body because the Holy Spirit lives there. Think of it thus: because the Holy Spirit lives in the material house of a believer, then every time a demon knocks at the door the Holy Spirit answers. Since God the Holy Spirit is stronger than any demonic being, including Satan himself, then no demon or evil spirit could enter. It's that simple: God is greater than Satan; thus, He protects His children.
>
> Jesus used the same analogy when he refuted the Pharisees: "When the unclean spirit goes out of a man it passes through waterless places, seeking rest, and does not find it" (Matt. 12:43). In this illustration, the demon is searching for a new home because he was cast out of the individual whom he once occupied. The word for "cast out," *exerchomai*, is the same word used of the departure of a demon in other possession

episodes. Then the homeless demon says, "I will return to my house from which I came" (v. 44). The demon and his friends can only enter the house if it is empty, that is, "unoccupied." Because the house is vacant, the demons entered, *eiserchomai*, another technical term for demon possession. In the case of all believers, the house is *occupied*, and God the Holy Spirit answers the door even if repossession is attempted. This passage is saying that only *empty* houses—unbelievers—can be reoccupied; therefore, Christians cannot be demon possessed. [3]

Mark Bubeck, an expert on demonology, agrees.

It is my conviction that no believer can be possessed by an evil spirit in the same sense that an unbeliever can. In fact, I reject this term altogether when talking about a believer's problem with the powers of darkness. A believer may be afflicted or even controlled in certain areas of his being, but he can never be owned or totally controlled as an unbeliever can...

The spirit of the Christian is reborn, regenerated, possessed, and sealed by the Holy Spirit in a way not enjoyed by the rest of man's being as yet. The spirit of man thus reborn, becomes the Holy Spirit's unique center of control and operation within man. I do not believe that any wicked spirit can ever invade a believer's spirit. [4]

The Spirit of God resides in the believer, and 2 Corinthians 3:17 says, "Where the Spirit of the Lord is, there is liberty." No demon can hold a believer hostage to the power of Satan. Robert Lightner summarizes the issue well.

I do not believe demons can indwell believers. Several reasons support the conclusion. First, none of the passages used to prove believers can be demon-possessed even use the words *demon* or *demons*. Second, none of those who were actually demon-possessed can be proven to be believers. Third, it is inconceivable that God the Father, God the Son, or the Holy Spirit would share their abode in believers with demons of hell. [5]

Scriptural Instruction

The numerous, unambiguous statements in Scripture about the relationship of Satan and demons to the believer in Christ are inconsistent with the idea of demons possessing believers. Here are three of the many examples.

- "He rescued us from the domain of darkness, and transferred us to the kingdom of His beloved Son" (Colossians 1:13). The rescue or deliverance of the believer from the domain of darkness is inconsistent with being possessed by a demon.

- "The Lord is faithful, and He will strengthen and protect you from the evil one" (2 Thessalonians 3:3). How could the Lord's protection of His children be reconciled with His allowing them to be demon possessed?

- "We know that no one who is born of God sins; but He who was born of God keeps him, and the evil one does not touch him. We know that we are of God, and that the whole world lies in the power of the evil one" (1 John 5:18-19).

There are several issues in this third passage, but the primary one that concerns us here is the statement "and the evil one does not touch him." In these verses, the evil one is Satan and his minions, and the one who is born of God is a believer in Christ. The word "touch" (*hapto*) in this verse means "to touch, take hold of, or hold." "This word indicates touch with intent to harm, which means Satan cannot touch or do any serious damage to the believer." [6] This would certainly include the most extreme form of damage to a Christian, which is demon possession. "It is hard to imagine how a believer could be demon possessed but also be said to have not been touched by the evil one." [7] Undoubtedly, 1 John 5:18 is another strong argument that clinches the view that a believer cannot be demon possessed.

Silence Interpreted

A third point against demon possession for believers is that the New Testament epistles are strikingly silent on this issue. I realize this is an argument from silence, but for me the silence speaks volumes.

> There is no clear example in the Bible where a demon ever inhabited or invaded a true believer. Never in the New Testament epistles are believers warned about the possibility of being inhabited by demons. Neither do we see anyone rebuking, binding, or casting demons out of a true believer. The Epistles never instruct believers to cast out demons, whether from a believer or an unbeliever. [8]

Think about it. If Christians can be demon possessed, then why do the New Testament epistles not warn us about it or instruct us about how to deal with the problem? It is unimaginable that the epistles, which were written to teach believers how to live vibrant, victorious lives until Christ comes, would omit something so important. [9]

Therefore, for these three reasons—Spirit indwelling, scriptural instruction, and the silence of the epistles—I don't believe that a Christian can be inhabited or indwelled by a demon.

The Spectrum of Demonic Activity		
General attack and temptation	Personal influence and oppression	Demon possession

◄─────────────────────────────────────►

Less direct and intense   More direct and intense

73

Should Christians today practice exorcism or deliverance?

In order to fully understand the New Testament teaching concerning casting out demons, let's briefly trace this topic through the Gospels, Acts, and the epistles.

Gospels

Eleven demon-related incidents are recorded in the first three Gospels. There are three general statements about casting out demons (Matthew 4:24; 8:16; Luke 7:21). This doesn't include the parallel passages that describe the same event. Added to that are eight specific incidents:

1. the demoniac of Gadara—Matthew 8:28-34 (Mark 5:1-20; Luke 8:26-39)

2. a mute man—Matthew 9:32-34

3. the Syrophoenician woman's daughter—Matthew 15:21-28 (Mark 7:24-30)

4. the boy with convulsions—Matthew 17:14-21 (Mark 9:14-28; Luke 9:37-42)

5. a blind and mute man—Matthew 12:22 (Luke 11:14)

6. a man in the Capernaum synagogue on the Sabbath—Mark 1:23-28 (Luke 4:33-37)

7. Mary Magdalene—Mark 16:9 (Luke 8:2)

8. a woman in the synagogue on the Sabbath—Luke 13:10-17

Strictly speaking, there are no exorcisms in Scripture. The word "exorcism" is never used of expelling a demon from a person. Exorcism refers to "casting out of evil spirits by conjurations, incantations, or religious or magical ceremonies."[1] The biblical term is to "cast out" (*ekballo*) a demon. The word "exorcist" appears only in Acts 19:13 and refers to some unsaved Jews who used magical rituals to attempt to expel demons.

The practice of casting out demons is related to the healing ministry of Jesus. It's a form of healing. The miraculous ministry of Jesus was a sign of His person. It authenticated Him as the promised Messiah. The scope and success of Jesus' healing ministry was astounding. The 70 who were sent out by Jesus in Luke 10 cast out demons, but they were given a special, limited commission by Jesus to go out ahead of Him to the cities He was about to visit. Their ministry was limited in time and geography. There is no evidence their special commission went beyond this limited calling.

Jesus warned that some who cast out demons in His name and performed many miracles in His name would be rejected in the day of judgment (Matthew 7:21-23). Casting out a demon or working a miracle does not prove that a person is a true believer. Satan is the master fraud.

Acts

The apostles cast out demons on three occasions in the book of Acts (8:5-8; 16:16-18; 19:11-12). In 19:11-12, the last recorded demon expulsion in Scripture, demons were cast out without any physical presence of an apostle or any command to depart in Jesus' name. "God was performing extraordinary miracles by the hands of Paul, so that handkerchiefs or aprons were even carried from his body to the sick, and the diseases left them and the evil spirits went out." Mere contact with Paul's sweat rags and apron resulted in deliverance from evil spirits. In Acts 5:15-16, people were healed, including deliverance from demons, by Peter's shadow. Who would imitate these methods today?

The only person besides the apostles who cast out a demon in Acts was Philip, who was an assistant to the apostles through the laying on of hands (Acts 6:5-6; 8:6-7). The book of Acts refers to demon expulsions as signs (Acts 5:12-16). In Acts 19:13, some unbelieving Jewish exorcists tried unsuccessfully to cast out demons in Jesus' name.

Epistles

Interestingly, the New Testament epistles never mention the practice of casting out demons. However, they do teach that miracles and healing, including casting out demons, were special identifying signs of an apostle. Paul reminded the Corinthians, "The signs of a true apostle were performed among you with all perseverance, by signs and wonders and miracles" (2 Corinthians 12:12). Signs and miracles must have been unique occurrences in order to authenticate that someone was an apostle. A sign must be distinct to be effective. If many people were performing signs and wonders, they would not have served as identifying signs of an apostle. This affirms their uniqueness.

The epistles affirm that the gift of apostleship was a temporary, foundational gift of the church that ceased in the first century (Ephesians 2:20). An apostle had to be a witness of Christ's life and resurrection and be personally commissioned by Him (Acts 1:21-22). Since this is true, when apostleship ceased, gifts of miracles and healing—the unique signs of apostleship, including casting out demons—also ceased. Of course, God still works miracles today and heals miraculously according to His sovereign will. He often works through and in response to the prayers of His people. But the divine enablement to perform miracles and healings as a gift possessed by a particular individual is not viable today. The book of Hebrews, written in the mid-60s, recognizes that signs and wonders were already a thing of the past (Hebrews 2:3-4).

Conclusion

Does the absence of instruction on casting out demons and the cessation of healing gifts with the apostles mean that believers today are helpless to assist a person who is demon possessed? I don't think so. I believe the norm today for delivering demon-possessed unbelievers is the preaching of the gospel. Evangelism is the means of exorcism.

> Upon belief in Christ as Savior, an unbeliever is delivered not only from his sin but also from any demon possession that might have afflicted him. So the proper biblical way to deliver an unbeliever from demons is to preach the gospel to him. It does not benefit the victim for someone to cast out demons (if possible) only to have him remain in his unsaved condition...Any believer can deliver another person from demons by leading him to Christ. The Scriptures do not require a second step of deliverance for a believer that he may be freed from the demonic powers; Christ sweeps the house clean at the moment of salvation and the Holy Spirit fills it. [2]

Here are seven scriptural conclusions about casting out demons.

1. Jesus and the apostles cast out demons from several unbelievers.

2. The 70, who were commissioned directly by Jesus for special, limited ministry, cast out demons.

3. Philip, who was in close contact with the apostles and experienced the laying on of hands by them, carried out a limited ministry of casting out demons.

4. Casting out demons was part of the unique healing ministry of Jesus that authenticated Him as the Messiah. It was also one of the confirming signs of true apostleship. Since apostleship has ceased (Ephesians 2:20), this form of deliverance from demon possession has also passed.

5. No established method or pattern of demon expulsion is presented in the New Testament.

6. The epistles contain no command or instruction concerning casting out demons.

7. Demon-possessed unbelievers today are set free by placing saving faith in Jesus Christ. Evangelism is the key that unlocks the door of deliverance—from sin and from Satan.

74

What are the signs that someone is demon possessed?

We can develop a kind of "possession profile" from the cases of demon possession in Scripture. While all of these symptoms may not always be present, these are ten manifestations of demon possession in the New Testament.

1. superhuman physical strength (Mark 5:3; Acts 19:16)

2. fits of rage and ferocious behavior (Mark 5:4)

3. high pain tolerance (Mark 5:5)

4. self-mutilation (Mark 5:5)

5. foaming at the mouth (Luke 9:39)

6. seizures or convulsions (Luke 9:42)

7. divided personality (Mark 5:6-7) (The demoniac ran to Jesus yet at the same time cried out in fear.)

8. resistance to spiritual things, especially the name of Jesus (Mark 5:7)

9. clairvoyance or supernatural knowledge (Mark 5:7; Acts 16:16)

10. change in voice (Mark 5:9)

75

Can people inherit demons or generational spirits?

The notion of generational spirits is that demon possession or occult practices can be inherited by children from their parents or other ancestors. All would agree that children inherit characteristics from their parents, but the idea of generational spirits or transference of demons is another issue altogether. Support for generational cursing is drawn from several Old Testament passages (Exodus 20:4-7; 34:6-7; Numbers 14:17-19; Deuteronomy 5:7-10). Those who believe in inherited curses or generational spirits maintain that if parents or grandparents engaged in occult practices, those practices must be uncovered and renounced to prevent the curse from being passed on to their descendants. They believe the inherited curse could even include demon possession.

All of the Old Testament passages used to support this are directed to the Jewish people and are part of the curses and blessings in the Mosaic covenant. Believers today are not under the curses of the Mosaic Law. In that day, parents who led their families into idolatry brought a curse upon their family—the covenant curses would follow their disobedience.

> You shall not make for yourself an idol, or any likeness of what is in heaven above or on the earth beneath or in the water under the earth. You shall not worship them or serve them; for I, the LORD your God, am a jealous God, visiting the iniquity of the fathers on the children, on the third and the fourth generations of those who hate Me, but showing lovingkindness to thousands, to those who love Me and keep My commandments (Exodus 20:4-6).

Notice that God's disfavor was broken for any member of the family who changed from loving idols to loving God and keeping His commandments.

> The nature of the curses in the Mosaic Law was to recognize that parents pass on certain traits and teach patterns of life to their children. When parents have rejected Christ and mire themselves in paganism, idolatry, and the occult, they teach these sins to their children. The result is the transfer of rebellion from one generation to another. But this fact does not remove from the subsequent generation their own responsibility for sin. In fact, the Bible teaches just the opposite. No matter what false religion is passed on by one generation to another, the children decide to accept or reject

it. They are punished ("cursed") for their own decision
to follow the rebellious path of their parents.[1]

This is illustrated time after time in the lives of the kings of
Judah. Often a good king had an evil son and an evil father had
a godly son. Each king reaped certain consequences from the
actions of his father, but each king was held responsible for his
own actions. No king was cursed for what his father did.

The Bible nowhere records the case of curses or generational
spirits that required exorcism or deliverance. The only curses in the
Bible that are treated as effective are those spoken by God Himself. God is faithful to carry out His curses as well as His blessings.

76

What is *tartarus*, and why are some demons there?

The term *tartarus* appears only once in the New Testament. "God
did not spare angels when they sinned, but cast them into hell
and committed them to pits of darkness, reserved for judgment"
(2 Peter 2:4). The words "cast them into hell" translate the verbal form of the Greek word *tartarus*. We could say the angels who
sinned were *tartarized*.

In Greek mythology, *tartarus* was the lowest part of the underworld. The demons who are imprisoned in *tartarus* cannot be
there because of their original sin of rebellion; otherwise, all the
demons would be there, including Satan himself. They also cannot be part of the group of fallen angels in the abyss in Revelation
9 who are released during the tribulation period because the angels
in *tartarus* are permanently bound there until the day of judgment. Moreover, *tartarus* and the abyss are two different parts of
the underworld.

So who are these fallen angels in *tartarus*? I believe they are the fallen angels ("sons of God") who sinned in Genesis 6:1-4. This interpretation is based on two main points. First, 2 Peter 2:1-8 lists three grave sins of the past: the sin of angels (2:4), the sin of the people in Noah's day (2:5), and the sin of Sodom and Gomorrah (2:6-8). These sins are all recorded in Genesis and are in chronological order. That means the sin of the angels preceded the sin of Noah's day. The only event recorded in Genesis that fits the sin of these angels is in Genesis 6.

Second, note the correlation between this passage and Jude 6, which says, "Angels who did not keep their own domain, but abandoned their proper abode, He has kept in eternal bonds under darkness for the judgment of the great day." Jude and 2 Peter 2 are strikingly parallel chapters, and the statement in Jude 6 confirms the Genesis 6 view of 2 Peter 2:4.

I believe 2 Peter 2:4 is a reference to a group of demons who assumed some human form and seduced women to cohabit with them. Due to the gross and shocking nature of this sin, these demons were confined immediately and permanently in *tartarus* until they are ultimately cast into the lake of fire.

77

Where are demons today?

We have touched on this issue already in several places, including the previous question, but it might be helpful to bring this all together in one place. The Bible teaches that there are two broad groups of demons: unconfined demons and confined demons.

Unconfined demons are free to roam the universe doing Satan's bidding. They are loose and active (Ephesians 6:10-12).

Confined demons can be further subdivided into three groups:

those bound permanently in *tartarus* for their sin (Genesis 6; 2 Peter 2:4; Jude 6), those bound temporarily in the abyss for going too far in their rebellion at some point (Luke 8:31; Revelation 9:1-9), and four fallen angels who are bound at the Euphrates River for an assignment during the end times (Revelation 9:14).

Thus, fallen angels can be found in four places today.

1. Some demons are unconfined and roam the universe (Ephesians 6:10-12).

2. Some demons go too far in sin and are temporarily confined in the abyss (Luke 8:31). They will be released for five months during the tribulation (Revelation 9:1-9).

3. Four demons are temporarily bound at the River Euphrates until they are released for a special mission (Revelation 9:14).

4. The angels who sinned in Genesis 6:1-4 are confined in *tartarus* until the day of their final judgment (2 Peter 2:4; Jude 6).

Part 3

The Invisible War and the Believer's "Armor All"

Spiritual warfare is not about the struggle of man against man. It is not a political struggle, a social struggle, or an economic struggle, or even a religious-theological-doctrinal struggle. It is not a struggle between human beings. It is a struggle within human beings... The battle is not against people, but against unseen spiritual powers. In fact, the entire human race is under a vicious assault by certain principalities and powers, world rulers of darkness, wicked spirits in high places... Every man, every woman, every child, everywhere is a target. The devil has each one of us in his crosshairs. The whole race is opposed by principalities and powers, the world rulers of this present darkness.

RAY STEDMAN

There is no truce in the invisible war. There is no armistice in the invisible war... There are hundreds of millions of battles being fought every day in the invisible war. The field of each battle is the heart of man.

DONALD GREY BARNHOUSE

A young football coach was hired as a scout for his college. Before his first assignment, he asked the coach what kind of player he was looking for.

The coach said, "Well, there is the kind of guy who when you knock him down, just stays down."

"We don't want him, do we, Coach?"

"No. Then there is the kind of guy who, when you knock him down, gets up. But if you knock him down the second time, he just stays down."

"We don't want him either, do we, Coach?"

"No, we sure don't. But there is the kind of guy who, when you knock him down, gets up; knock him down, and he gets up; knock him down, and he gets up; knock him down again, and he just keeps getting up every time."

"That's the guy we want, right, Coach?"

"No, we don't want him, either. We want the guy who is knocking all the other guys down."

We can all say amen to that. It's wonderful that by God's grace we can get up and start over again every time the enemy knocks us down. But it's even better to keep from getting knocked down or even to be spiritual victors who knock the enemy back.

78

What is spiritual warfare?
Are we really in a war?

John F. Kennedy was a commissioned naval officer during World War II. His patrol boat, the PT 109, was rammed and sunk by an enemy destroyer near the Japanese-held Solomon Islands in August 1943. Kennedy and a fellow officer swam from one enemy-occupied island to the next until they found some friendly islanders who helped them contact US forces. Years later, Kennedy was hailed as a war hero, but his candid response was, "It was involuntary. They sank my boat."[1]

So it is with every believer. We don't have to volunteer to find ourselves engaged in a war. It's involuntary—the war has come to us. Satan and the world rage against us without, and our flesh opposes us within. Some seem to believe that coming to Christ removes them from the battle, but the opposite is true. The battle really begins when a person becomes a Christian. Every believer in Christ is in the midst of an invisible war. Scripture reminds us, "Suffer hardship with me, as a good soldier of Christ Jesus" (2 Timothy 2:3). As Erwin Lutzer says, "We're in a war. We can't plead pacifism. We can't run from the bullets. We can't hide from the bombs. We can't plead medical deferment."[2] There are two sides in this cosmic war of the ages. "The enemy is Satan, the battleground is our mind, and the issue is our Christian walk. We do not live in a neutral world. There are hostile forces at work in it, an evil one with a host of helpers opposed to God and to man."[3]

Winston Churchill once said of Kaiser Wilhelm that he wanted to be Napoleon without fighting Napoleon's battles. The Kaiser wanted victories without wars. Don't we all? Especially in the

Christian life. But it's just not possible. There are no victories without battles. We don't live in a neutral world. [4]

The phrase "spiritual warfare" never appears in the Bible. It's a theological, practical term for describing the conflict of the Christian life. The spiritual battle we're facing is an epic struggle pitted against Satan and his angels, against the principalities and powers. It is being fought every day right where we live—in our homes, our offices, our marriages, our church, and in the inner core of our hearts. Billy Graham describes the spiritual war that rages.

> We live in a perpetual battlefield—the great War of the Ages continues to rage. The lines of battle press in ever more tightly about God's own people. The wars among nations on earth are merely popgun affairs compared to the fierceness of battle in the spiritual, unseen world. This invisible spiritual conflict is waged around us incessantly and unremittingly. Where the Lord works, Satan's forces hinder; where angel beings carry out their divine directive, the devils rage. All this comes about because the powers of darkness press their counterattack to recapture the ground held for the glory of God. [5]

John MacArthur defines spiritual warfare as...

> a war of universal proportions pitting God and His truth against Satan and his lies. It's a battle of wills between God and Satan. It's a cosmic conflict that involves God and the highest creature He ever made, and it filters down to every human being. Satan and his army of demons are fighting Christ, His holy angels, the nation of Israel, and believers. The battle lines are clearly drawn. [6]

Spiritual warfare is the invisible war waged in the spiritual realm but fleshed out in the visible, physical realm. [7]

Ephesians 6:10-20 is the classic New Testament text on spiritual warfare. We could call it the believer's field manual for spiritual warfare. The ancient metropolis of Ephesus was swarming with occult activity. Paul's initial visit there sparked an encounter with demonic powers in which Christ's name was proven supreme (Acts 19:11-20). Many of the believers in Ephesus had been steeped in the occult before coming to Christ.

In Ephesians 5:22–6:9, Paul addresses several specific groups within the church (wives, husbands, children, fathers, and slaves). In 6:10 he addresses the entire congregation again, warning them and us about the spiritual war we all face. It's instructive that the section on spiritual warfare follows the section on the family in Ephesians. This is no accident. Satan's attack on marriages and the family is real and relentless. As someone has said, "When you get married, that's when the war begins."

Ephesians 6 tells us that the invisible world around us is just as real as the visible world, and it's filled with demonic terrorists who want to undermine our faith and hinder our spiritual progress. Ephesians 6:12 identifies the intensity and scope of the conflict. "Our struggle is not against flesh and blood, but against the rulers, against the powers, against the world forces of this darkness, against the spiritual forces of wickedness in the heavenly places." The Greek word translated "struggle" was originally used for wrestling, which was part of the Greek games. The picture of wrestling highlights the immediacy and closeness of the conflict and the effort and stamina required.

The word "against" occurs six times in Ephesians 6:10-18, spotlighting the cosmic clash of forces and the intensity of the struggle. The Lord wants us to know what we're up *against*. The battle lines are clearly drawn. God and His people are on one side, and Satan and his demons are on the other.

"Flesh and blood" refers to people. This is not saying that we have no struggle against other people (on the human level), but that our struggle is not *just* on that level. The ultimate conflict in spiritual warfare is waged against the spiritual forces of darkness that are at work behind the *seen*.

79

What is the Christian's strength for the battle against demons?

Following the second Battle of Alamein in the early days of World War II, Winston Churchill delivered one of his famous speeches. At one point he said, "Now this is not the end. It is not even the beginning of the end. But it is, perhaps, the end of the beginning." What was true at Alamein is also true in many ways of the Christian life. Conversion is not the end of the Christian struggle. It is not even the beginning of the end—it's just the end of the beginning. A lifetime of spiritual conflict will follow.[1] For this reason, every believer needs to understand God's battle plan against the enemy.

Ephesians 6:10 introduces the first prong of this battle plan: Our only true resource in the struggle against the powers of darkness is the Lord's power. "Be strong in the Lord and in the strength of His might."

The Greek verb translated "be strong" (*endunousthe*) is a present passive imperative. This means the strength comes from God (passive voice); it is to be a continual, habitual part of the believer's experience (present tense); and it is absolutely necessary if victory is to be realized (imperative mood). Ephesians 6 uses three words for power (empowered, strength, might), which highlights the truth that every child of God has accessibility to divine power.

As 1 John 4:4 states, "Greater is He who is in you than he who is in the world." Second Chronicles 20:15 reminds us, "The battle is not yours but God's." Our Commander in Chief has won the war. Christ defeated the enemy at the cross. We fight a defeated foe. Power comes from the Lord, not our own ingenuity or methods. Of course, we are not inactive. Scripture commands us to stand and resist the enemy. We should give maximum effort to follow the Lord's commands and put on the full armor He provides.

A friend of mine visited a Navy Seal installation in California, and he saw a large plaque that says, "The enemy thanks you for not giving 100 percent today." Our enemy is pleased when we fail to give 100 percent, but he is also pleased if we give 100 percent and rely only on our own strength. God uses our efforts, but they are insufficient. We must be strong in Him.

S. Lewis Johnson says, "You notice the Apostle does not say, 'be strong in human plans.' He does not say, 'be strong in human methods.' He does not say, 'be strong in the latest ideas that sweep over the evangelical church, but 'be strong in the Lord and the power of His might.'"[2] We need the Lord. We don't need Him and something else. We need Him. George Duffield wrote these stirring words years ago:

> Stand up, stand up for Jesus,
> Stand in His strength alone;
> The arm of flesh will fail you,
> Ye dare not trust your own.

80

Who are the three enemies of every Christian?

In the 1700s, on the island of Cape Hatteras off the shore of North Carolina, a group of men lured ships aground on the shoals just off the island. The men, known as "wreckers," made their living gathering up the wreckage and cargo of the ships. Their strategy was to fasten a lantern to the head of an old horse (a "nag") and then walk the nag up and down the shore just outside their village, which was appropriately known as Nag's Head. Out at sea in the blackness of the mid-Atlantic night, ships that were searching for a passage past the islands would mistake that bobbing light for the stern light of a ship they supposed had found safe passage. They would steer inland and run aground on Diamond Shoals, and their ship would break apart. In the morning, the wreckers would come to the shore and salvage timber for new houses, utensils for their kitchens, and money for their wallets. It was a thriving business. Today, visitors to Nag's Head can see old houses built and furnished with material taken from the more than 2300 ships that met their demise off this coast either by accident or treachery.

When we first hear about these Nag's Head wreckers, we're shocked and angry. Who would do something so sinister and greedy? But we might be far more shocked and indignant if we realized that we are constantly being stalked and lured by much more malicious spiritual wreckers who are constantly working behind the *seen* to shipwreck our lives.[1]

Who are these wreckers? According to Scripture the spiritual wreckers every believer faces every day are the world, the flesh, and the devil. This is the terrible triumvirate of foes that seeks to shipwreck the spiritual life of every follower of Christ and hold unbelievers in the darkness to keep them from experiencing the warmth and light of Jesus Christ. Spiritual warfare rages on three fronts: by land (the flesh), by air (demons), and by sea (the world). We have discussed Satan and demons at length already, but we need to define the other two wreckers.

The World

The first enemy believers face is the world (Greek, *kosmos*). In modern usage, the term "world" often refers to an organized set of ideas, people, activities, and purposes, such as the world of sports, the world of politics, or the world of finance. In the same way, in the Bible, the world is the prevailing false system of values and beliefs in society.

> Worldliness is an organized and attractive system of ideas, concepts, attitudes and methods that Satan uses to compete with God's concept of how people should live on planet Earth. Satan is the head and controller of this system of thinking...
>
> The *cosmic* system is Satan's window dressing, presenting evil in a way which seems like the good, right and proper thing to do.[2]

Lewis Sperry Chafer, the founder of Dallas Theological Seminary, describes the world system.

> The *cosmos* is a vast order or system that Satan has promoted which conforms to his ideals, aims, and methods. It is civilization now functioning apart from God—a civilization in which none of its promoters really expect God to share, who assign to God no consideration in respect to their projects. This system embraces its godless governments, conflicts, armaments, and jealousies, its education, culture, religions of morality, and pride. It is that sphere in which man lives. It is what he sees,

what he employs. To the uncounted multitude it is all they ever know so long as they live on this earth. It is properly styled *the satanic system*...It is literally a *cosmos diabolicus*.[3]

The world system is fully unveiled in 1 John 2:15-17.

Do not love the world nor the things in the world. If anyone loves the world, the love of the Father is not in him. For all that is in the world, the lust of the flesh and the lust of the eyes and the boastful pride of life, is not from the Father, but is from the world. The world is passing away, and also its lusts; but the one who does the will of God lives forever.

Worldliness is often defined in terms of certain behaviors, such as gambling, going to certain movies, wearing certain kinds of clothes, and so on. But worldliness goes much deeper. It's a mindset, or attitude. Of course, this attitude reveals itself in actions, but worldliness begins as an attitude. A concise definition of worldliness is a love for passing things.

The three facets of the world system in 1 John 2:16 are the lust of the flesh (the desire to satisfy the impulses of the flesh), the lust of the eyes (the desire for things we see), and the boastful pride of life (the desire to promote self). E.M. Bounds graphically portrays the world system that surrounds us.

The world includes the mass of humanity that is alienated from God and therefore hostile to the cause of Christ. It involves worldly affairs, earthly things, riches, pleasures, and pursuits that are shallow, frail, and fleeting. These things stir desire, draw us away from God, and are obstacles to the cause of Christ...

The world is the Devil's heaven. Its rest, crown, and reward are here. When the world comes in, God's heaven goes out. It fades from the eye and heart. The struggle for it ends, and God's heaven, with its fadeless and eternal glories, is lost.[4]

The world tempts us to covet its treasures, crave its power and prestige, and conform to its standards.

The Flesh

The flesh (Greek, *sarx*) is our sinful nature. It's often described as a principle, influence, or nature. Regardless of the specific term, it is a predisposition to assert our own will against the will of God. Every person knows what it is—it is the traitor within, the principle of sin and disobedience that resides within every person (Romans 7:14,18; Galatians 5:13-21). It is the seat of self-centeredness within us that never improves. It's the "urge within us toward total autonomy and rebellion, toward being our own little gods— accountable to no one, responsible to no one…running our own little worlds to suit ourselves."[5]

In Galatians 5:19-21, the apostle Paul graphically exposes the symptoms of the flesh.

> Now the deeds of the flesh are evident, which are: immorality, impurity, sensuality, idolatry, sorcery, enmities, strife, jealousy, outbursts of anger, disputes, dissensions, factions, envying, drunkenness, carousing, and things like these, of which I forewarn you, just as I have forewarned you, that those who practice such things will not inherit the kingdom of God.

Now that we have defined the world and the flesh, let's see what the Bible says about overcoming these stubborn foes.

81

How do believers gain victory over the world?

The clear teaching of the New Testament is that God's people are not to love the world, but are to separate from it.

- "Do not be conformed to this world" (Romans 12:2).

- "The grace of God has appeared...instructing us to deny ungodliness and worldly desires" (Titus 2:12).

- "Pure and undefiled religion in the sight of our God and Father is...to keep oneself unstained by the world" (James 1:27).

- "Friendship with the world is hostility toward God" (James 4:4).

- "You may become partakers of the divine nature, having escaped the corruption that is in the world" (2 Peter 1:4).

- "They have escaped the defilements of the world" (2 Peter 2:20).

- "Do not love the world" (1 John 2:15).

To separate from the world, however, is not to withdraw from it or rigidly avoid certain activities, but to allow God to transform your mind, to begin thinking the way He does. The only way to not love the world and to avoid its conforming, squeezing influence is to be transformed. Romans 12:2 says, "Do not be conformed to this world, but be transformed by the renewing of your mind." According to this verse, every person is either being conformed or transformed. You might ask yourself right now, "Which is true of me? Am I being conformed or transformed?"

The Greek word translated "transformed" is *metamorphoo,* from which we get our word "metamorphosis." This word is used in Matthew 17:2 of the transfiguration of Jesus, when what was on the inside burst through on the outside. The word *metamorphoo* in Romans 12:2 is an imperative, present tense, passive verb. That means we are commanded to constantly be allowing our lives to be transformed by God.

So how does this transformation occur? By the renewing of your mind. Change on the outside begins on the inside. The process of renewing the mind is also described in 2 Corinthians 3:18, where the word *metamorphoo* appears again. "We all, with unveiled face, beholding as in a mirror the glory of the Lord, are being transformed into the same image from glory to glory, just as from the Lord, the Spirit." The mirror is the Word of God. When the child of God looks into the Word of God, the Spirit of God transforms that believer over time into the image of the Son of God. A transformed, renewed mind is saturated with and focused on God's Word. And it turns a deaf ear to the siren call of the world.

82

How do believers overcome the flesh?

Some years ago I read about a psychiatric hospital that devised a simple yet effective test to determine whether patients were ready to be released. A candidate for release was brought into a room where a faucet was turned on, gushing water all over the floor. The patient was given a mop and instructed to mop up the water. Patients who took the mop and just started mopping away with the water still flowing remained in the hospital for additional treatment. But those who had the sense to first turn off the faucet and then mop up the water were ready to go back into society.

No sane person would leave the water running, but sadly, many Christians live their spiritual lives in this absurd fashion. God has given each believer a mop to help clean up the messy world around us, but we can only succeed if we first have enough sense to shut off the flow of sin that pours from our own hearts. We can be of little or no help cleaning up the moral and social problems of our culture as long as we remain a part of the problem. We have to turn off the flow of sin from our own flesh before we can minister to a world in desperate need of cleansing.[1] Scripture sets forth a two-pronged battle plan against the flesh.

Flee

The first facet of the plan against the flesh is simply to flee. Sins of the flesh are subdued by running away. First Corinthians 6:18 says concisely, "Flee immorality." Second Timothy 2:22 says, "Now flee from youthful lusts and pursue righteousness, faith, love and peace, with those who call on the Lord from a pure heart." You don't win the fight with the flesh by standing and slugging it out. You'll get knocked out every time.

Joseph is the classic example of this. When Mrs. Potiphar worked her charms on him, he didn't try to talk her out it, reason with her, or stand there trying to decide what to do—he ran for his life. All he left behind was his coat. As the old saying goes, he lost his coat but kept his character. The only way to win over gluttony is to get the food out of the house. Get the ice cream out of the freezer. Pornography is not defeated by dabbling around with it. Sexual immorality is not avoided by hanging around. You have to run.

Follow

The second strategy for fighting the flesh is to follow the Spirit. Galatians 5:16-17 says, "Walk by the Spirit, and you will not carry out the desire of the flesh. For the flesh sets its desire against the Spirit, and the Spirit against the flesh; for these are in opposition to one another, so that you may not do the things that you please." This passage pictures the vicious battle between two warring parties that is raging inside every believer—the battle between the flesh, or sin nature, and the Spirit. The battle is won by walking in the Spirit, or depending on Him.

The image of walking pictures the daily life of the believer. Walking by means of the Spirit pictures moment-by-moment dependence. Consider people who use walkers to get around. When they use a walker, they walk. The walker doesn't walk for them. They have to put one foot in front of the other, but they depend on the walker. They walk by means of the walker, or in reliance upon it.

When a believer depends on the Spirit, the sin nature is impotent. The Greek in Galatians 5:16 contains a double negative that could be translated, "Walk by the Spirit, and you will by no means, ever fulfill the desire of the flesh." But the moment a person chooses to depend on himself, he falls under the control of the sinful nature and begins to walk "according to the flesh."

Every believer must choose moment by moment either to surrender to the impulses of the flesh or to depend on the Spirit. H.A. Ironside told the story of a simple man who was trying to explain the conflict of the flesh and the Sprit. He said, "It seems to me as though two dogs are fighting within me. One is a black dog, and he is very savage and very bad. The other is a white dog, and he is very gentle and very good. But the black dog fights with him all the time."

Someone asked the man, "And which dog wins?"

He replied, "Whichever one I say 'sic him' to."

That's true. If a believer feeds the flesh, the flesh will triumph, but if he depends on the Holy Spirit, the Spirit will control. The Spirit is constantly leading every believer (Romans 8:14; Galatians

5:18). "The issue is not whether we are being led, but whether we are following." [2]

———— 83 ————

How can we know whether temptation is coming from demons, the world, or our own flesh?

Undoubtedly, there is some overlap and cooperation between the three enemies of the believer. Satan and demons take full advantage of the world and the flesh to stymie any spiritual progress. But how can we know if a problem or temptation has gone beyond a fleshly or worldly temptation and crossed over into the demonic arena? I don't believe there's any pat answer to this question, but Mark Bubeck's comments are insightful.

> The answer to this seems again to rest in this matter of sound doctrine. If I earnestly seek the defeat of one of the fleshly sins through the biblical methods previously discussed but without results, if I find a worldly temptation defeating me even though I am aggressively using my provided victory over the world, I must now consider the fact that my problem well may be some demonic hold of Satan's powers which must be broken.
>
> Spiritual warfare includes a continual, active aggressive warfare against all three enemies. I must seek to understand which enemy I am facing that I might apply God's remedy against that enemy. It is not good to blame our own fleshly depravity on the world or even on Satan.[1]

I agree with Bubeck, but I would add that neither is it good to blame the world or Satan for sin that finds its genesis in my own flesh. Absent some strong evidence to the contrary, the best place to begin when we are tempted or afflicted is with our own flesh. But as Bubeck observes, if we follow the biblical commands for gaining victory over the flesh and the issue persists, we move to the world and then to the demonic as a final resort. Prayer should be part of this process of elimination as we seek God's enlightenment and energizing to diagnose the source of our trouble or temptation and achieve the victory.

84

Is it biblical for Christians to rebuke Satan and demons?

Popular books, articles, seminars, and TV preachers often encourage Christians to engage in offensive, aggressive forms of spiritual warfare, including binding and rebuking Satan and demons. Many well-meaning but misled Christians have bought into this approach despite the fact that believers are never enjoined in Scripture to seek out or attack Satan or demons.

We don't need to seek them out; they seek us out. Simply read the New Testament epistles. You will find nothing even close to "instructing Christians to seek out, speak to, defy, deride or cast out demons."[1] Jude 9 says that even Michael the archangel did not rebuke Satan when arguing with him over the body of Moses. I can't find anywhere in Scripture where believers are told to talk to Satan or demons. Rather, we are to talk to God in prayer (Ephesians 6:18-20).

Jesus did not rebuke or bind the devil when He faced him in the wilderness. "When Satan came against Him with three fiery temptations, Christ did not enter into an extended dialogue. Neither did he condemn or bind the Devil. He responded by using the sword of the Spirit (Matt. 4:1-11)." [2] We should follow the example of our Master.

85

What are binding and loosing?

Have you ever heard someone say, "I bind the works of the devil," or "Satan, I bind you and release God's blessings." Have you ever wondered where they got the idea for this practice?

After Peter gave his great confession of Christ, Jesus said, "I will give you the keys of the kingdom of heaven; and whatever you bind on earth shall have been bound in heaven, and whatever you loose on earth shall have been loosed in heaven" (Matthew 16:19). Jesus repeated the same thought in Matthew 18:18 in the context of church discipline. "Truly I say to you, whatever you bind on earth shall have been bound in heaven; and whatever you loose on earth shall have been loosed in heaven."

The key word that many seize on in these verses is "bind" (Greek, *deo*). The words "binding" and "loosing" here denote the idea of "forbidding" and "permitting." The religious leaders of Jesus' day used the terms in this way. In the context of Matthew 16 and 18, binding and loosing have nothing to do with Satan or demons. The binding refers to the actions of other people, not the devil or demons.

The passages in Matthew are saying that believers have the authority on earth to act in conformity with God's Word, knowing that when they judge on the basis of God's Word, they can rest assured that their judgment corresponds with the judgment of heaven.[1]

The terms "binding" and "loosing" are judicial. We bind (forbid) on earth what has already been bound in heaven and loose (permit) what has already been loosed in heaven. We carry out God's will on earth as it has already been determined in heaven.

86

Do good angels help believers in spiritual warfare?

Speaking of angels, the writer to Hebrews says, "Are they not all ministering spirits, sent out to render service for the sake of those who will inherit salvation?" (Hebrews 1:14). There are many illustrations of angelic ministry to God's people in Scripture, but I will mention two dramatic examples that are related to spiritual warfare.

As we have already seen, Daniel 10 reveals that the answer to Daniel's prayer was interrupted by demons, and Michael the archangel and another unnamed good angel waged war with them to see that the answer to the prayer was delivered.

Another striking example of angelic assistance is found in 2 Kings 6, where the king of Aram came to Dothan to capture the prophet Elisha.

> Now when the attendant of the man of God had risen early and gone out, behold, an army with horses and chariots was circling the city. And his servant said to him, "Alas, my master! What shall we do?" So he answered, "Do not fear, for those who are with us are more than those who are with them." Then Elisha prayed and said, "O LORD, I pray, open his eyes that he may see." And the LORD opened the servant's eyes and

he saw; and behold, the mountain was full of horses
and chariots of fire all around Elisha (2 Kings 6:15-17).

The king of Aram was no doubt influenced by demons to try
to get rid of the great prophet of Israel. Eliminating Elisha would
have been a great score for Satan. However, when the enemy army
arrived, Elisha was surrounded by a host of heavenly horsemen
who protected him. Although we cannot look behind the cur-
tain into the unseen world, we can rest assured that God employs
angels to minister on our behalf as well and protect us from the
enemy.

87

Do territorial spirits control cities and nations, and should Christians identify and pray against them?

One approach to spiritual warfare that has gained ground in recent
years centers on the ideas of territorial spirits, spiritual mapping,
and identificational repentance. Adherents to this viewpoint assert
that evangelistic efforts are deterred by evil spirits who dominate
specific geographical turf. The main proponent of this concept is
C. Peter Wagner. Proponents of this view identify three levels of
spiritual warfare, with the highest level being "strategic."

> Strategic-level spiritual warfare requires power confron-
> tations with high-ranking principalities and powers as
> described by Paul in Ephesians 6:12. These demonic
> entities are assigned to geographical territories and
> social networks. They are also referred to as territo-
> rial spirits. Their assignment is to keep large numbers
> of humans—networked through cities, neighbor-
> hoods, regions, nations, people groups, industries,

governments, businesses, education systems, religious alliances, media, or any other form of social institutions—in spiritual captivity.[1]

An integral part of this level of warfare is a process called "spiritual mapping," which is "a process by which the specific territorial spirit(s) of an area is discerned and named."[2]

> Spiritual mapping is the practice of identifying the spiritual conditions at work in a given community, city, or nation. By gathering objective information (including key historical facts such as foundational history, locations of bloodshed, idolatrous practices, key historical leaders, broken covenants, and sexual immorality) and combining it with spiritual impressions (prophecy, revelation, words of knowledge, dreams, and visions), believers can prayerfully combine all of this information and draw a map that identifies the open doors between the spirit world and the material world. These open doors help determine our response as we enter into warfare prayer.[3]

No one disputes that Satan has a hand in blinding the minds of lost people and holding them in unbelief. "The whole world lies in the power of the evil one" (1 John 5:19). The question is whether Satan has a hierarchy of demons who rule specific territories, whose identities must be discovered, and whose power must be bound prior to successful gospel outreach.

Many serious objections to this methodology could be raised, but the principal problem with this view is that the Bible doesn't support it. Nothing even close to spiritual mapping or power encounters with territorial spirits is found in the pages of Scripture. Daniel 10 does mention demons who are identified with certain ancient nations (Persia and Greece) and a spiritual turf war over these nations with good angels. But this is a far cry from the elaborate strategy that modern spiritual warriors have concocted.

Daniel 10 simply tells us that demons are highly organized, that they fight with good angels, that they exercise influence over world governments, and that they can interrupt the answers to the prayers of believers. Nothing in Daniel 10 supports identifying territorial spirits or spiritual mapping. The good angel that addresses Daniel tells him that he must go help Michael the archangel, who is continuing the fight against demons, but he never solicits Daniel's help in any way. Daniel is never told to do anything, let alone identify the evil spirits or engage in the kind of praying against territorial spirits that is encouraged by many today. Strategic-level spiritual warfare and spiritual mapping have no biblical precedent. Nowhere in Scripture are believers instructed to command demons to give up any territory.

> A marked difference stands between the nature of Daniel's prayer and what is presently termed "strategic-level intercession." Daniel never sought the names of these cosmic powers nor did he employ their names in his intercession—a practice more in keeping with occultic arts. In fact there is no indication that Daniel was aware of what was taking place in the heavenlies during his three-week period of prayer and fasting. It is not until *after* this period that Daniel received revelation about the identity of the angels engaged in this heavenly struggle. And even then, the only angel who was named was Michael (10:13), who fought on behalf of Israel...
>
> Also Daniel did not engage in aggressive prayer against such powers with the expectation of "binding" or "evicting" them. The prophet did not pray *against* cosmic powers but *for* the people of God and

the fulfillment of God's redemptive purposes (cf. Eph. 6:18-20). Apparently Daniel's focus in prayer was not on the celestial warfare in the heavenlies, but on the promises of God (Dan. 10:12; cf. Jer. 25:11; 29:10) and their fulfillment on the terrestrial scene. [4]

Wayne Grudem highlights four main problems regarding territorial spirits.

> In no instance does anyone in the New Testament 1) *summon a "territorial spirit"*…2) *demand information from demons about a local demonic hierarchy*, 3) *say that we should believe or teach information derived from demons*, or 4) teach by word or example that certain *"demonic strongholds" over a city have to be broken* before the gospel can be proclaimed with effectiveness. [5]

In His letter to the church of Pergamum in Revelation 2:13, Jesus said that Satan dwelled there and even had his throne there. Yet interestingly, Jesus did not instruct the believers there to rebuke, bind, or identify the evil spirits or command them to leave the city. His main message to them was to repent of their compromise with the world.

One could argue not only that it is unwarranted for believers to command demons to give up spiritual territory but that it actually plays into the hands of demons by sidetracking believers into wasting time and energy on unbiblical practices. Timothy Chester says it well:

> Spiritual warfare is not about naming territorial spirits, claiming ground or binding demons. It is all about the gospel. It is to live a gospel life, to preserve gospel unity and to proclaim gospel truth. It is to do this in the face of a hostile world, a deceptive enemy and our

own sinful natures. And it is to pray to a sovereign God for gospel opportunities. Advance comes through godliness, unity, proclamation and prayer. [6]

These things should attract our focus, not unbiblical, mystical practices.

88

Is the intensity of spiritual warfare the same all the time?

Someone once said that the problem with the Christian life is that it's so *daily*. This is especially true in the case of our spiritual warfare. Sometimes God's people can get weary in the fog of war, but Scripture tells us that it is not continuously uniform in its intensity. Although the battle is daily, not all days are the same. The enemy doesn't keep coming at us with the same consistency and intensity every day. Ephesians 6:13 says, "Therefore, take up the full armor of God, so that you will be able to resist in *the evil day.*"

Believers are always under attack by the enemy. Life is an unrelenting spiritual struggle from the cradle to the grave. We might call this everyday evil. But there are also "times of heightened and unexpected spiritual battles."[1] These times of especially furious attack by the enemy are called the "evil day." There are seasons when the evil escalates, when pressures are more intense, when the problems, trials, and temptations seem to gang up on us all at once, and when the intensity of the struggle is ratcheted up.

Satan prowls around for vulnerable prey (1 Peter 5:8). The enemy waits, watches, and probes for times when we are weak and vulnerable. The evil day is when the enemy mounts an all-out attack against you. When he throws on the full-court press. It's the day when your number comes up.

> The evil day is the day that all hell breaks loose in your life—when you are under attack. It's when the finances are so low, you don't know how you are going to make it through the end of the week. It's when you've lost your job, and there is no new job in sight. It's when you are breaking down emotionally and have lost your passion for life. It's when your marriage seems hopeless, your kids have turned away, your health deteriorates, or your future looks bleak. It's when your friend has betrayed you, you're overcome by an addiction or impulse, or life seems to deliver any other piercing stab.[2]

I read a quote somewhere once from Alexander MacLaren that describes these times of all-out attack. "They are the days when all the cannons fire at once, and scaling ladders are reared on every side of the fortress." Ask Job about the evil day. The time when Satan unleashed everything he had against Job. Peter faced the evil day when Satan sifted him like wheat (Luke 22:31-32). Jesus faced the evil day in the wilderness when He was tempted for 40 days. The devil left until an opportune time, which he found later when Jesus was in dark Gethsemane. To those who came to arrest Him, Jesus said, "While I was with you daily in the temple, you did not lay hands on Me; but this hour and the power of darkness are yours" (Luke 22:53).

The powers of darkness are looking for an opening to bring the evil day in our lives, our homes, our marriages, and our churches. The evil day will come for every believer at some point in our lives. It will come for you; it will come for me. Our only defense is to take up the full armor of God and hold our ground in the strength of the Lord. We are more than conquerors through Him.

89

How do we resist the devil?

All three of the believer's enemies—the world, the flesh, and the devil—are mentioned in James 4:1-7. As we have seen, different strategies help us achieve victory over these enemies.

- the flesh—*flee* from sin and *follow* the way of righteousness (1 Corinthians 6:18; Galatians 5:16,18; 2 Timothy 2:22)
- the world—*focus* on God's Word (Romans 12:2; 1 John 2:16)
- the devil—*fight* (Ephesians 6:10-12; James 4:7)

When it comes to dealing with the devil and his demons, believers are never commanded to bind, rebuke, curse, or deride them. But we are told three times in the New Testament to resist the devil (Ephesians 6:13; James 4:7; 1 Peter 5:9). James 4:7 says, "Submit therefore to God. Resist the devil and he will flee from you." The Greek word translated "resist" (*antihistemi*) means "to stand against" or "to oppose," which emphasizes the defensive posture of the believer.

The battle plan for winning over demonic attack is to resist, to stand firm, to hold our ground, to fight. If we effectively resist the devil he will flee. The Greek word translated "flee" in James 4:7 is *pheugo*, from which we get our word "fugitive." We can send the enemy on the run if we resist him. But how do we resist the devil in our everyday lives? What does that look like?

Scripture provides three keys to resisting and withstanding the assaults of the enemy. First, we must submit to God and draw near to Him. James 4:7-8 says, "Submit therefore to God. Resist the devil and he will flee from you. Draw near to God and He will draw near to you." Submitting yourself to God must come before resisting the devil. Every Christian ought to cultivate two views with all that he has: the devil's back and the face of God. The only view more welcome than the backside of the devil as he flees is the face of God. God wants us to submit and draw near to Him. That's the first step in effectively resisting the devil.

The second practical step in resisting the devil is to cultivate a humble heart. James 4:7, which commands us to resist the devil, is bracketed by verses 6 and 10, which both mention humility. This signals to us that humility is essential to resisting the devil. The more humble we are, the less impact the forces of evil can have upon us. We give them less to work with. As Jonathan Edwards said, "Nothing sets a man so much out of the devil's reach as humility." Resisting the devil does not mean rebuking him by shouting at him. It refers to a lifestyle of submission and humility.

> We cannot have victory over the greatest of all rebels if we ourselves are rebels. God resists those who side with Satan in pride (James 4:5-6). We are to humble ourselves and submit to God. Then we can resist the devil and he will flee from us...Our lives must be His. The measure of our submitting provides the basis of our resisting, and the measure of our resisting determines the measure of the devil's fleeing. [1]

The third step in resisting Satan is to put on the full armor of God. Ephesians 6:13 says, "Take up the full armor of God, so that you will be able to resist in the evil day, and having done everything, to stand firm." Putting on our spiritual body armor enables us to resist the devil and stand against him. First Peter 5:8-9 says, "Your adversary, the devil, prowls around like a roaring lion, seeking someone to devour. But resist him, firm in your faith." We resist the enemy by standing firm in our faith, which parallels the shield of faith in Ephesians 6. That brings us to a consideration of the armor of God.

90

What is the full armor of God?

During World War I, British Admiral Lord David Beatty commanded a flotilla at the Battle of Jutland. As the battle commenced, British and German ships engaged each other in long-range artillery fire. It quickly became apparent that the British ships had a major flaw. First, a heavy cruiser, the *Lion*, was hit by an artillery barrage and quickly sank. Next the *Indefatigable* was hit in the powder magazine and blown to pieces. Then the *Queen Mary* was sunk, taking a crew of 1200 sailors to the bottom of the sea. As Admiral Beatty watched the destruction of his ships, he turned to his bridge officer and said with the characteristic British restraint, "There seems to be something wrong with our ships today, Chatfield."

Though the British ships eventually turned back the German fleet, it was later discovered that the British ships did have a fatal flaw. Though they had heavily armored hulls, their wooden decks offered almost no protection against long-range enemy artillery shells, which dropped almost straight down out of the sky. Only after the British began to armor their ships on top as well as on the sides did they stop losing ships to German long-range artillery.[1]

Effective armor is crucial for victory in any war—including spiritual warfare. If God's people leave anything unprotected, the enemy will find a way to exploit the chink in the armor and bring destruction. According to Ephesians 6, God has provided complete weaponry or combat gear, called the "full armor of God," so every believer can resist the attacks of the enemy. The full armor of God leaves nothing uncovered or unprotected. The words "full armor" translate one Greek word (*panoplia*), which is found three times in the New Testament (Luke 11:22; Ephesians 6:11,14). The *panoplia* was the complete battle gear of a heavily armed Roman foot soldier, known as a hoplite. The six-piece full combat gear is issued to every believer by the Holy Spirit at the moment of conversion. We will consider each piece of this armor later. It's what I like to call the believer's "Armor All."

1. the belt of truth

2. the breastplate of righteousness

3. the shoes of peace

4. the shield of faith

5. the helmet of salvation

6. the sword of the Spirit

The image of spiritual armor for the believer is found in the Old Testament in Isaiah 11:4-5 and 59:16-17. Paul also certainly adapted this image from his own time in prison by observing the soldiers who constantly kept watch over him and at times were chained to him. Paul's audience could relate to this image and understand it easily.

The words "full armor" indicate that every item is essential. We can't pick and choose. It's the full armor—the complete panoply. Martyn Lloyd-Jones emphasizes this point.

> If you are to be a soldier in this army, if you are to fight victoriously in this crusade, you have to put on the entire equipment given to you. That is a rule in any

army…And that is infinitely more true in this spiritual realm and warfare with which we are concerned… You need it all—"the *whole* armor of God"—because your understanding is inadequate. It is God alone who knows the enemy, and He knows exactly the provision that is essential to you if you are to continue standing. Every single part and portion of this armor is absolutely essential; and the first thing you have to learn is that you are not in a position to pick and choose.[2]

The apostle Paul further indicates that the full armor of Ephesians 6 is "of God." This means it's the armor God provides. It's not man-made or manufactured. It is His armor. God's people must rely daily on supernaturally provided combat gear for this spiritual battle. Believers have access to God's power by means of this armor, but victory is not automatic. We must put on the armor (Ephesians 6:11), or take it up (verse 13), in order for it to be effective. Every believer must appropriate it into daily life. God *makes* the armor, but the Christian has to *take* the armor. We need all the armor all the time if we're going to stand firm.

One way to think about the armor of God is to view it as a picture of our Lord. Romans 13:12-14 says, "The night is almost gone, and the day is near. Therefore let us lay aside the deeds of darkness and *put on the armor of light…Put on the Lord Jesus Christ,* and make no provision for the flesh in regard to its lusts." Notice that putting on the armor of light is equivalent to putting on the Lord Jesus Christ. He is our armor.

Jesus is the belt of truth, for He is the way, the truth, and the life. He is the breastplate, for He is our righteousness. He becomes our shoes of peace, because He is our peace. He is the shield of faith, for He is the author and finisher of our faith. And He is the helmet of salvation, for we are told in the Bible that we have the mind of Christ. We are to wear Christ the way we wear our clothes.

"Clothes are with us all the time, always visible, and become a natural part of our lives. So also should Christ always be a part of our everyday living. When we put on the armor, we are putting on Christ and going forward in His strength to do battle." [3]

91

What is the purpose of the armor of God?

I come from Oklahoma, where football is part of our lifeblood. It's been well said that football is warfare with rules. Football serves as an interesting analogy of spiritual warfare. In football, the players put on their "full armor" before the game, including a helmet, pads, and shoes. The players must also have a clear game plan, must understand the tactics and tendencies of their opponent, and must stay in close contact with the head coach. Football, like spiritual warfare, also requires character and stamina, and it is a game of both individual and team effort.

One of the most compelling features of football is the goal-line stand, when a defense is backed up in the shadow of its own goalpost. The defenders dig in for a gritty, down-and-dirty struggle in the trenches and refuse to budge. They make a stand. They refuse to yield an inch of ground. A victorious goal-line stand is often the turning point in a game. Nothing takes the starch out of an offense like getting stopped cold on four consecutive plays at the opponent's one yard line.

Likewise, in spiritual warfare, it is crucial that we learn how to make a successful stand and refuse to yield any ground to the enemy. [1] Many today have the mistaken idea that believers are to go on the attack to storm the gates of hell. They think in terms of charge, advance, and gaining new ground. They wonder, "Does God really expect me to just stand?"

The answer is yes. That's what the Bible says. Jesus has achieved the victory for us already. He has won the war and gained the spiritual ground staked out in Ephesians 1–3. Now it's up to us to hold the spiritual ground He gained on our behalf. We must not yield, but instead remain immovable and withstand the onslaught of the enemy. The purpose of the armor is not to gain new territory. We fight *from* victory, not *for* victory.

The word "stand" punctuates this passage.

> Put on the full armor of God, so that you will be able to *stand* firm against the schemes of the devil…Therefore, take up the full armor of God, so that you will be able to resist in the evil day, and having done everything, to *stand* firm. *Stand* firm therefore, having girded your loins with truth, and having put on the breastplate of righteousness (Ephesians 6:11,13-14).

Similar statements are found elsewhere in the New Testament.

- "Resist the devil and he will flee from you" (James 4:7).
- "Resist him, firm in your faith" (1 Peter 5:9).

A strong defense will win the day. Our best offense is a good defense. Lewis Sperry Chafer said it well: "As pilgrims we *walk*, as witnesses we *go*, as contenders we *run*, as fighters we *stand*."

92

When are we to wear the armor of God?

I have had the privilege of visiting the Holy Land on three occasions. I can honestly say that I never felt safer. The Jewish people live with constant awareness that they are in an ongoing state of conflict. War could break out any day even though everyone is always talking about peace. The Israelis live with the ever-present reality of conflict, so they take that into consideration with everything they do. On the streets, civilians are practically surrounded by Israeli soldiers and security forces. The nation lives in a constant state of military readiness because its leaders and people understand they are living on a battleground.

Several years ago, I saw a group of school children on a field trip up in the area of Dan in northern Israel. The teachers had automatic rifles slung over their shoulders. Even with this hypervigilant readiness, they suffer some casualties, but imagine what would happen if they let their guard down and lived as if they had no enemy.

This highlights one of the reasons we see so many spiritual casualties in the church. We have lost sight of the fact that we are in a perpetual state of spiritual warfare that is as dangerous as any physical conflict and that demands our constant alertness and vigilance. We dare not let down our guard. We cannot become complacent. God has provided us with resources to win this war, but we must avail ourselves of His provision at all times.

In question 88, we discussed the "evil day," or the time when the enemy launches an all-out assault against us. We don't know when that day is coming, so we must always be ready. We need to wear all the armor all the time.

Ephesians 6:11,13 uses different words for "putting on" and

"taking up" the armor, but both verbs are in the aorist tense, which stresses urgency as well as permanence (keep it on). We never know when the enemy will strike, so it's imperative to be prepared at all times.

Several years ago in my home state of Oklahoma, a sheriff's deputy in a nearby county was shot four times in the chest at point-blank range during a routine traffic stop. His bulletproof vest saved his life. In the story in the paper, he said that his three children remind him every day to wear his bulletproof vest. He said, "Every day when I leave the house, one of them says, 'I love you Dad. Don't get dead.'" Law enforcement officers must put on their body armor every morning. They never know when the attack will come—when a routine traffic stop will turn into an all-out assault. The only way to be prepared is to always wear the armor.

John de Courcy was a strong and courageous Anglo-Norman knight who arrived in Ireland in 1176 and conquered a considerable amount of land. He was a devout worshipper and always gave God the glory for his victories. King John of England wanted him killed but knew it would be difficult because de Courcy was such a fierce warrior.

King John commissioned Sir Hugh de Lacy to find out how to capture and kill de Courcy. To learn about de Courcy's habits and weaknesses, de Lacy conferred with certain of de Courcy's own men as to how he might be taken, and they said it was not possible to take him because he always wore his armor. The only time each year when he took off his armor was Good Friday. His custom on that day was to wear no armor and carry no shield or weapon. He walked around the church five times barefoot and then spent the rest of the day in church, kneeling in prayer.

De Lacy determined that Good Friday was the only opening to kill de Courcy, so on that day a group of his men descended suddenly upon him. De Courcy found nothing but a cross pole to defend himself and killed 13 men until it broke. Finally, with no armor and no weapon, the great warrior was captured. The enemy found his weakness and struck when he had taken his armor off. In the brief time when he was defenseless, the enemy attacked.

Our enemy is no different. We can be sure that he knows when we're not wearing our armor. We have to put it all on, all the time. Without it we're easy prey.

93

What is the belt of truth?

Having discussed the armor in general, let's look now at each individual piece. The armor is listed in Ephesians 6:14-20, which is one 113-word sentence in Greek. Warren Wiersbe aptly calls this section, "what to wear to the war."

The first piece of equipment the Roman hoplite put on to go to war was his belt. No soldier could fight without his belt. The soldier's belt was six inches wide and constructed of leather or linen. The belt served two main purposes. First, the soldier used the belt to gird his loins, that is, to tuck his tunic into it so he could move freely and fight effectively without tripping. Second, it supported his weapons. The ordinary solider hung his sword from it. The archer used it to support his quiver of arrows. The belt held everything else together. In the same way, truth holds everything together for the child of God. Truth must come first.

Many excellent Bible teachers define truth here as truthfulness, or the believer's personal integrity. Undoubtedly this is a key to life and protects us against the enemy, but I don't believe that's the primary emphasis here. Remember, the armor in Ephesians 6 is not man-made. It's the armor *of God*. It's His armor, which He provides for us. Personal integrity is an inadequate defense against satanic forces.

I see the belt of truth as a reference to God's objective truth. This fits well because God's truth enables us to move freely and holds everything else together. Also, truth would logically be the first item mentioned because Satan is a deceiver, the father of lies. Our first weapon against the great deceiver and liar is God's unchanging truth. It never requires updating. It never needs to be modernized.

> Truth is reality. Truth is the sum total of the way things really are. Therefore, truth is the explanation of all things. You know you have found the truth when you find something wide enough and deep enough and high enough to encompass all things. That is what Jesus Christ does.[1]

During the days of World War II, Allied forces employed a massive campaign of deception that is still studied today. It preceded the invasion of Normandy and was known as Operation Fortitude. The purpose of this campaign was to lure the Germans to commit their resources to places other than Normandy. In various places, inflatable tanks, plywood artillery, and other decoys were constructed and put in key locations to keep the German forces occupied. The main part of the deception was false wireless traffic by German double agents. The deception worked beautifully. The Germans were distracted from the concentration of forces that invaded Normandy on D-Day.

Satan is engaged in a massive campaign of deception. Successful spiritual warfare is not a matter of mastering complicated techniques or vocabulary. It's knowing the truth of God and applying it to your daily life. God's truth has already been provided for us, but we have to take it up, put it on, and internalize it.

Since truth is our chief weapon against deception, Satan's chief strategy is to attack God's Word, which contains the truth. Satan's oldest trick is to subtly discredit the Word, distort it, and then defiantly deny its inspiration and infallibility. His first words in Genesis 3:1 were "Has God said?" If Satan can attack God's Word successfully, he can undermine our faith and sabotage our spiritual progress and maturity. He attacks the truth and the sufficiency of Scripture.

How do believers put on and cinch up the belt of truth? By knowing God's truth. Here are some practical ways to ensure that your belt is firmly in place.

- Attend church regularly to hear instruction from God's Word.

- Listen to faithful preachers on the radio, CDs, or podcasts.

- Read, study, and meditate on God's Word.

- Participate in a good Bible study.

- Memorize the Word.

I love the story of the man who went to visit his old friend, a music teacher, and casually asked, "What's the good news today?"

Without saying a word, the elderly music teacher walked across the room, picked up a tuning fork, and struck it. As the clear tone sounded, the old man said, "That note is A. It is A today, it was A a thousand years ago, and it will be A ten thousand years from now. The soprano upstairs sings off-key, the tenor across the hall flats his high notes, and the piano downstairs is out of tune. But this…" He struck the note again. "This, my friend, is A, and that's the good news for today." [2]

That is the good news of Jesus Christ. He is the truth, the same yesterday, today, and forever. He is the One to whom we can tune our lives. His truth stands. His Word is the truth today. It was truth a thousand years ago, and it will be truth ten thousand years from now. We have found the One who is the solid, unchanging Rock. Cling to Him and His truth. If you have never believed in Him and received Him, you need to come to Him today—the way, the truth, and the life. Surround your life with the belt of truth.

All the verbs and pronouns in Ephesians 6:14-20 are in the plural, which means, of course, that the passage applies to every believer. But it also indicates to us that we aren't alone. We're in God's army together. We're a band of brothers and sisters. We are struggling side by side, arm in arm, shoulder to soldier. We stand for God's truth together. This should serve as a great encouragement to each of us. Seeing others standing firm and resisting the devil shores up our own faith and gives us the resolve to do the same.

94

What is the breastplate of righteousness?

No Roman soldier entered battle without a breastplate. It was a tough, sleeveless piece of armor that covered his full torso. It was made of leather or heavy linen with overlapping slices of animal hooves or horns or pieces of metal sewed on it. Some were made of large pieces of metal molded or hammered to conform to the body. The breastplate protected the heart, lungs, and other vital organs.

Similarly, righteousness protects our heart against the accusations and condemnation of the enemy. Righteousness has to do with both *being* right and *doing* right. It's what we are and what we do.

Righteousness in this context can refer to subjective, sanctifying righteousness, often called practical righteousness, or it can refer to positional righteousness. Most commentators take the first view. In other words, they affirm that a righteous, obedient life is our defense against the enemy.

No one would disagree that living a righteous life guards the heart of a believer against the assaults of the devil. But I favor the idea of Christ's righteousness as the *primary* emphasis in our breastplate while recognizing that practical righteousness will result from a right position.

The Bible tells us that when we become believers in Christ, His righteousness is credited to our heavenly bank account, and we are declared righteous before God. In 1 Corinthians 1:30 we read, "By His doing you are in Christ Jesus, who became to us wisdom from God, and righteousness and sanctification, and redemption."

When Jesus hung on the cross, two monumental things happened. First, He took all our sin upon Himself. He became sin for us. Second, He imputed His righteousness to us. When we trust Him, He forgives all our sins and gives us His righteousness. We become righteous in Him. No one could imagine a greater bargain. Christ takes my sin and gives me His righteousness.

The theological term that describes our righteousness in Christ is *imputation*, which is an accounting or banking term that means to credit to a person, to reckon over to one's account, to put to someone's account. My favorite verse, 2 Corinthians 5:21, expresses this truth. "He made Him who knew no sin to be sin on our behalf, so that we might become the righteousness of God in Him." We could call this the great exchange. He gets our sin, and we get His righteousness.

I learned a great deal about transference or imputation when my sons were in college and graduate school. My wife and I were constantly transferring money to their accounts—crediting our funds to their account. They didn't earn the money, so why did we credit our money to their account? We did it because they're our sons, and we love them dearly. Why does God transfer or impute Christ's righteousness to our heavenly bank account? Because we deserve it or work for it? No. Because we are His sons and daughters through faith in Jesus Christ, and He loves us.

The transfer of Christ's righteousness occurs the moment you believe in Christ and put your trust in Him. Based on this transaction, God declares you justified, or righteous before Him (Romans 5:1). One of Satan's great tactics is to attack our hearts with false accusations. When you put on the breastplate of righteousness, you allow the righteousness of Christ to protect you from enemy assaults. Romans 8:33 reassures us, "Who will bring a charge against God's elect? God is the one who justifies."

Martin Luther urged Christians to make the truth of Christ's righteousness a part of their daily prayers by saying, "Thou, Lord Jesus, art my righteousness, but I am thy sin. Thou has taken upon thyself what is mine and hast given me what is thine. Thou hast taken upon thyself what thou wast not and hast given to me what I was not."[1] Anglican theologian Richard Hooker (circa 1554–1600) said, "We care for no knowledge in the world but this, that man hath sinned, and God has suffered; that God hath made himself the sin of men, and that men are made the righteousness of God."[2]

Christ is our righteousness. We rest in His merits—in His righteousness alone. Standing before God accepted and not condemned gives us great strength and should result in a life of practical righteousness. When Satan accuses you before the Lord and points out all your faults and failures, God the Father says, "I see him clothed in the righteousness of My Son, Jesus Christ." This is our strong defense against demonic accusations. Christ's righteousness is our impenetrable breastplate.

95
What are the shoes of peace?

At one point in the Academy Award–winning movie *Forrest Gump*, Forrest strikes up a conversation with a nurse sitting next to him on a park bench. After admiring her shoes for a few minutes, he says, "My momma always said you can tell a lot about a person by their shoes. Where they're going. Where they've been."

Shoes play a significant role in our lives. There are all kinds of shoes for every conceivable kind of activity. Go to any mall and visit the athletic shoe stores or the shoe department of any large department store. There are stylish shoes, expensive shoes, and different kinds and colors of shoes for any kind of sport or style one can imagine. Athletic shoes are constantly changing to implement the newest technology and scientific breakthroughs. Imagine a football team with the best state-of-the art equipment but with no shoes or with shoes with no cleats. Proper footwear is critical.

Not surprisingly then, the next piece of armor the soldier depended on in battle was his shoes—"…and having shod your feet with the preparation of the gospel of peace" (Ephesians 6:15). A soldier's shoes are even more important than an athlete's because his life depends on them. The image in Ephesians 6 comes from the Roman soldier's war boot, known as the *caliga*. One Roman Caesar was known as Caligula, which means "little boots."

The caliga was the half-boot worn by Roman legionnaires. It was an open-toed leather boot that was tightly fastened to the ankles and shins with leather straps. The boot was stuffed with wool or fur in cold weather. These shoes weren't for running (pursuing or fleeing from the enemy). These thick-soled boots were made for long marches and for a solid stance to enable the soldier to keep his footing during close combat. The leather sole was three-quarters of an inch thick, and the bottom was studded with hollow-head hobnails so the fighters could make quick, sudden moves without slipping and falling. [1] Envision a Roman soldier in armor from head to foot but with no shoes. A barefoot soldier would quickly tear his feet and would easily lose traction. He would be out of action in no time. Nothing else matters if you can't keep your footing.

Commentators interpret this reference to the shoes of peace in two ways. First, some maintain that it is an encouragement to share the good news of the gospel of peace with others—that believers must be ready each day to share the gospel of peace with a lost world. This view contends that the shoes of peace represent a readiness to make the gospel known. Those who hold this view note that the most victorious Christian is a witnessing Christian. In support of this, they point to Romans 10:15, which says, "How will they preach unless they are sent? Just as it is written, 'How beautiful are the feet of those who bring good news of good things!'"

Preaching the gospel and sharing our faith are important, but I do not believe that's what this verse is talking about. Paul doesn't say that our feet are shod with the *proclamation* of the gospel of peace, but with the *preparation* (readiness) of the gospel of peace. Also, remember that the armor is defensive, not offensive (except the sword of the Spirit).

I think the better view is that the soldier's shoes refer to our peace with God through the gospel, which makes us immovable. Scripture tells us that before a believer comes to Christ, he is an enemy of God, at war with the Creator. But when a sinner trusts Christ as Savior, he is instantly justified by faith, and the result is peace with God (Romans 5:1,10). Jesus is the Author of peace. He is God's peacemaker (Ephesians 2:13-14). This is the gospel of peace, which gives us firm footing. Every believer now enjoys an eternal, settled peace with God. And this new position empowers Christians to resist the devil.

People who don't know if they have peace with God are unstable and weak and easily tripped up by the enemy. They slip all over the place. With feet firmly planted in the peace of God, they can weather and withstand the greatest assaults of the enemy.

96

What is the shield of faith?

Ephesians 6:16 mentions the fourth piece of God's "Armor All"— the shield of faith. The shield is introduced by the words "in addition to all." In addition to all the other pieces of armor, make sure you take up the shield.

There were three kinds of Roman shields. One was the small, round shield called a *clypeus*. We often see these in movies, such as *Gladiator*. The second, the one referred to in Ephesians 6, was the large oblong or oval shield called a *thureon*, which was derived from the word *thura* (door). The largest shield, called a *scutum*, was four feet tall, two and a half feet wide, and a hand's breadth in thickness. With hooks on each side, it could join to the shields of fellow combatants to form a solid wall of protection. Harold Hoehner describes the Roman shield.

> It was made of two wood planks glued together with the outer surface covered first with canvas and then with calf skin. There was metal on the top and bottom edges to protect the wood when it hit the ground, and on the center front there was an iron boss causing most stones and heavy arrows to glance off. [1]

Before battle, the shields were often immersed in water, soaking the leather cover and canvas beneath the leather to extinguish flaming arrows.

Movies like *300* depict large groups of ancient archers shooting their arrows at the same time. The shower of shafts blacken the sky. In the same way, the glowing shafts of Satan are constantly raining down on God's people. The shield is essential to extinguish these arrows.

After one ancient battle, a Roman soldier counted 220 darts sticking into his shield. The Roman shield was a key part of his defense. None of the other pieces mattered if he had no shield. For the believer in Christ, this protective shield is faith, or personal, daily trust in the Lord. Faith is vibrant trust in the promise and power of God.

Translating the Bible for a South Seas tribe, missionary John Paton discovered the people had no word for faith. One day a native who had been running hard came into the missionary's house, flopped down in a large chair, and said, "It feels so good to rest my whole weight in this chair." Paton said, "That's it. I'll translate faith as 'resting one's whole weight upon God.'" [2] That's a great definition of faith. Faith is resting our whole weight on God. It's the one thing that covers all the other weapons. Resolute faith enables believers to stand firm and resist the devil (1 Peter 5:9).

The shield represents faith, so the darts it extinguishes must include doubt. Satan's subtlest dart is doubt. It was the first dart he fired against Eve (Genesis 3:1), and he has been unloading the chambers ever since. The devil loves to double down on doubt.

Many Christians panic when they have the slightest doubt and wonder if they are really believers. But remember, doubt is not the opposite of faith. Unbelief is the opposite of faith. When doubt comes, stand against it in the truth you know. When we trust God concerning the truth we know, God will take care of what we don't know.

Finally, remember that the shield had edges that were constructed so that an entire line of soldiers could interlock shields and form a solid wall of protection. This suggests we are not in the battle alone. We're in God's army together. We are struggling side by side, shoulder to soldier, shield to shield. This should be a great encouragement to our faith. Sometimes spiritual warfare makes us feel alone. Seeing others standing firm and resisting the devil shores up our own faith and gives us the resolve to hold on.

97

What is the helmet of salvation?

The Roman soldier's helmet was made of bronze or iron and was lined inside with felt or sponge. It protected the brain—the mind. The mind of every believer needs the protection of our divine headgear. We live in confused times. We're constantly bombarded with news and events that can easily drive us to discouragement and even despair. People everywhere feel it. Satan seizes upon this to bring hopelessness. In an increasingly corrupt and confused world, every Christian needs to think clearly. Nothing is more important than keeping our thinking straight.

All of us who are believers in Christ have the helmet of salvation, which protects our minds and keeps us thinking straight in confused times. Salvation in the Christian life has three tenses:

> past—justification
>
> present—sanctification
>
> future—glorification

Which is in view here? I do not believe Paul is talking about the past tense of salvation because the previous two pieces of armor refer to that—the breastplate of righteousness and shoes of peace. I believe this looks primarily to the future, final aspect of our salvation. This is what Paul refers to in Romans 13:11 when he says, "Salvation is nearer to us than when we believed." The helmet of salvation is further defined for us 1 Thessalonians 5:8 as "the hope of salvation." Salvation in this context is a hope, something still in the future. This future tense of salvation is described further in Romans 8:22-25. The helmet of salvation pictures the coming of Jesus Christ, the day when He will deliver creation from bondage and establish His kingdom on earth. On that day, He will set things right and bring in righteousness, peace, and full salvation.

We who are God's people aren't to put our hope in political solutions, social programs, or scientific advances to solve the problems of this world, as helpful as those things sometimes are. Our hope is in Christ alone. Though we have no ultimate hope in humanity, we have every hope in God. This doesn't mean we withdraw from the world and isolate ourselves from its problems. We need to maintain our balance. We need to be involved in meeting the desperate needs of people in the depths of their pain and loss. God forgive us if we are uncaring or uninvolved in the pain and upheaval of our world. Yet our hope is not in humanity.

John MacArthur encourages us that our confidence is in our full salvation to come.

> Knowing there is an end to spiritual warfare provides motivation for persevering in battle. We will not have to fight the world, the flesh, and the devil forever...Living without hope would be like running a race without a finish line...If there were no guarantee of future salvation, the past aspect would be meaningless.[1]

The only thing that can keep our thinking straight and give us hope is remembering that Christ is coming again to bring our salvation to completion, that He is coming to save us and set things right, and that He alone can bring utopia on earth. Keeping this eternal plan in view will keep you from a great deal of heartache and fear as you read the paper every morning and listen to the news. It will keep you from being surprised, panicked, and stampeded by the relentless Niagara of disheartening information.

The hope of salvation reminds us that the battle is not ours, but the Lord's. History is not a meaningless mess, but rather a controlled plan that is right on schedule. Despite all appearances, Christ is directing these events, and everything will work out in the end. Nothing that happens can delay or upset His plan. For this reason, I believe it's imperative to preach and teach on the Lord's coming and biblical prophecy. God's people need regular reminding that Christ is coming again to bring our salvation to its consummation. It reminds us that the end is certain. The outcome is sure. It keeps our hearts and minds calm and undisturbed in the day of battle.

Today, when people are highly interested in the future and feeling a sense of hopelessness, teaching about the Lord's coming is less talked about than ever before. That's a shame because our hope is the helmet of salvation, which protects our minds from the confusion, chaos, and hopelessness of our times. "With our minds securely protected by the helmet of the ultimate salvation of God, we can face the evil days ahead with our thoughts ordered, our hearts calm, and our souls undisturbed by the trumpets of war." [2]

May our heads and hearts be full of hope until He comes!

98

What is the sword of the Spirit?

The final essential piece of the Roman soldier's panoply was his sword. Think of a Roman soldier with all his armor on and carrying a shield but with no weapon in his hand with which to attack the enemy and defend himself. He would quickly be cut down. Likewise, the Christian warrior must have a weapon for the war against Satan, and that powerful weapon is "the sword of the Spirit, which is the word of God." To help us understand this image, let's consider three key points: the sword, the Spirit, and the saying.

The Sword

The Bible includes many metaphors for the Word of God:

lamp (Psalm 119:105)

fire (Jeremiah 20:9)

hammer (Jeremiah 23:29)

water (Ephesians 5:26)

mirror (James 1:22-25)

seed (1 Peter 1:23)

One of the most common New Testament metaphors for Scripture is the sword (Hebrews 4:12; Revelation 1:16; 2:12,16; 19:15). There are two New Testament words translated "sword." One is *romphaia*, which was used for the Roman broadsword. The word translated "sword" in Ephesians 6:17, however, is the Greek word *machaira*, which refers to the Roman short sword. It was basically a large knife with a two-edged blade two inches wide and six to eighteen inches long. It was used in hand-to-hand combat. This tells us something about the conflict in spiritual warfare. It's up close. This is our offensive weapon, although in up-close fighting, one could just as easily view it as part of the defensive posture of holding ground.

This offensive quality of God's Word explains why the Word of God is under relentless attack. Satan has declared war on the Word of God because he knows its power. He influences some unbelievers to attack it, ridicule it, and undermine its significance. Satan speaks through people of prominence and intelligence to blunt, twist, disable, and discredit the testimony of Scriptures. Satan's strategy is to keep human beings from taking God's Word seriously. He even uses pastors in pulpits to water it down or even deny it. Even some so-called theology professors betray the Scriptures with the kiss of Judas. As an old saying laments, "If you're looking for Satan in the church, the place to start is the pulpit." Satan attacks the Word because it's our sword—our great offensive weapon. He fears its cutting edge. The Word of God cuts, convicts, challenges, confronts...but it also comforts. It's razor sharp. As someone has said, "It's all edge." It's the sword of the Spirit.

The Spirit

The second key point is the Spirit. Our weapon is the sword *of the Spirit.* The Spirit inspired God's Word. He is the author of it (2 Samuel 23:2; 2 Timothy 3:16; 2 Peter 1:21). The Word is a sword, and it's from the Spirit (that's its origin). That's why it's so powerful and valuable. Since the Spirit is the divine author of the Word, we can't separate the Word from the Spirit. We need Him to fill us and teach it to us.

When I attended Dallas Theological Seminary, the first semester was preceded by a few days of orientation. During one of the sessions, Donald Campbell, who was then president, made a comment I have never forgotten. He said, "Dallas Seminary has a faculty of One," referring to the teaching ministry of the Spirit. The

Spirit wrote the textbook, and He's the teacher. The sword we wield is His sword. The better our knowledge of the Scriptures and the deeper our fellowship with the Spirit, the more victorious we will be in the battle.

The Saying

The Word of God is a sword, and the Word of God is from the Spirit. That brings us to the saying. Two New Testament Greek words are translated as "the Word" of God.

The first is the familiar Greek word *logos*, which refers to the total utterance or revelation of God. The second and lesser-known word is *rhema*, which denotes a specific saying or verse of Scripture that applies to an immediate situation. The word *rhema* is the term used in Ephesians 6:17. In other words, when we face temptation or some other assault of the enemy we must counterattack with a passage or saying of Scripture that meets the situation head-on. God's wisdom in His Word is available for us in specific situations. The Bible is like an armory, and inside are all kinds of swords you can pull out when you need to cut down the enemy.

Jesus modeled this for us in the wilderness when He was tempted by Satan. We might call Matthew 4:1-11 the original Desert Storm. Satan chose his moment carefully. He came to Jesus right after His baptism and the approval of the Father from heaven, probably hoping to catch Jesus off guard at a susceptible time right after His great success. But our Lord was more than up to the challenge, deftly thrusting the sword of the Spirit and slicing up Satan in their duel in the desert. Faced with each temptation, He reached into His sheath and pulled out a sharpened sword. Christ, the Divine Warrior, is the Master Swordsman. Three times the sword flashed and sliced: "It is written…it is written…it is written."

Jesus quoted from the book of Deuteronomy each time. When I was a student at Dallas Seminary, one of my professors, Howard Hendricks, once posed this searching question: "If your spiritual survival depended on how well you knew the book of Deuteronomy, how long would you last?" Also, think about this. If Jesus used Scripture in His encounter with the enemy, how much more should we? James Boice asks the question this way:

> Here is Jesus—the holy Son of the Almighty God, the one in whom neither Satan nor man could find any wrong or gain even the tiniest foothold. Jesus' eyes were always on the glory of his Father. He lived in the closest possible communion with him. But if Jesus, your Lord and Savior, needed to know Scripture in order to resist Satan and win the victory over him, how much more do you and I need it to win a corresponding victory! We must know it word for word. You say, "Well, I have a general idea of what the Bible is about." That is a start, but it is not enough. You must know the Bible well and have key parts of it memorized if you are to overcome temptation…To be useful to us, the Bible's word must be yours and mine specifically. [1]

Boice then illustrates his point by referring to swords he has seen in his travels.

> Some were ornate. Some were historically significant, having belonged to kings or other influential people. Some were large, some were small. I enjoyed looking at them, but they have never done me any good, nor will they. They are not mine. I cannot hold them. They are locked away in great museums, and they will remain there. For a sword to do me any good, it would have to be mine. I would have to take it up and use it…only the words of God we actually know will be useful to us in living for God and overcoming temptation. [2]

The account of Satan's attack against Jesus closes with these triumphant words: "The devil left Him" (Matthew 4:11). Jesus resisted the devil, and he fled (James 4:7). We face the same battle and the same enemy that Jesus faced. We have the same choice. We can enjoy the same victory. It all depends on our knowledge and use of our sword. "I have written to you, young men, because you are strong, and the word of God abides in you, and you have overcome the evil one" (1 John 2:14).

When Virginia seceded from the nation, joining its Southern colleagues in confederacy, Stonewall Jackson's duty was plain. The time had come to fight and defend his native state and soil. Jackson stated briefly at an assembly of the cadets at Virginia Military Institute, "The time of war has not yet come, but it will come, and that soon; and when it does, my advice is to draw the sword and throw away the scabbard." Where is your sword all week? Is it safely in the sheath, sitting on the shelf? Or is it unsheathed and ready to use?

The lore of King Arthur includes a captivating story about the Lady of the Lake presenting the famed sword Excalibur to him. The sword was engraved on opposite sides: "Take me up...cast me away." That's the same choice every believer faces every day with our Excalibur—the Word of God. We can take it up or cast it away. Our spiritual survival depends in great measure on which choice we make.

99

How does prayer relate to spiritual warfare?

In modern warfare, establishing air superiority is critical. Whoever controls the air controls the war. If you establish air superiority, you'll suffer far fewer casualties on the ground, and you'll dominate your enemy. Sadly, the church today is suffering massive spiritual casualties on the ground because we haven't established superiority in the air—in the heavenly places, where the real warfare is taking place. The way we achieve air superiority is through prayer—by flooding the heavens with our prayers. That's spiritual air superiority. That's the key to victory.

The significance of prayer to spiritual warfare is evident in the very first word of Ephesians 6:18. The word "with" is a connecting word. Prayer is vitally connected to the discussion of spiritual warfare and the Christian's armor in 6:10-17. Our defense is not to speak to the devil or demons by binding or rebuking them, but to pray to God.

Ephesians 6:18-20 comes right on the heels of eight verses that deal with spiritual warfare and our arsenal of six pieces of armor. We might say that after describing our spiritual battle dress or what to wear to the war, Paul now tells us how to get dressed. We get dressed for battle in an attitude of prayer. The third stanza of the hymn "Stand Up, Stand Up for Jesus," written by George Duffield, captures the thought.

> Put on the gospel armor,
> Each piece put on with prayer;
> Where duty calls or danger,
> Be never wanting there.

We are never free from the battle, so we should never be long without prayer. An old Dutch proverb says, "What is heaviest must weigh heaviest." We have to allow prayer to weigh heaviest in our daily lives if we are to stand effectively for Christ and the gospel. James Boice offers this reminder:

> Our secret resource is prayer. And what makes it so important is that the weakest Christian can at any period of his life at any moment of the day and in any circumstance cry out to God for help and instantly have the resources of the infinite, sovereign God at his disposal.[1]

Dr. John Walvoord once told me a story about talking to the president of a well-known Bible college. When Dr. Walvoord asked his friend how things were going, he said, "We're going forward on our knees." We fight the battle on our knees. If we fight from any other position, we will surely suffer defeat. As John MacArthur says, "Ephesians begins by lifting us up to the heavenlies and ends by pulling us down to our knees."[2] God wants us to know that even though He has blessed us with staggering spiritual resources, we must still depend upon Him. Ephesians 6:18-20 describe six aspects of what I like to call "warfare prayer."

Varied Prayer

"With all prayer and petition." The word "prayer" refers to general requests, while "petition" refers to specific ones. The use of both words indicates that all kinds of prayer are in view.

Continual Prayer

"Pray at all times." Every believer should have set times each day to pray. For me, it's in bed in the morning and in bed at night. I like to wake up talking to the Lord and go to sleep talking to Him at rest in His strong arms. But prayer should be carried forward throughout the day. The rest of the day should be punctuated by prayer (Nehemiah 2:4; 1 Thessalonians 5:17). Praying at all times means we live in a state of continual God-consciousness.

Spirit-Directed Prayer

"In the Spirit." The third aspect of our warfare prayer is that it must be Spirit led. Praying in the Spirit does not mean praying in tongues or some kind of prayer language or ecstatic utterance. Praying in the Spirit is praying with His help and guidance (see Romans 8:26-27; Jude 20).

Vigilant Prayer

"And with this in view, be on the alert." Vigilant prayer is awake and alert, with eyes wide open. Don't just go through the motions. This echoes Jesus' words to Peter, James, and John in Gethsemane (Matthew 26:37-41).

Persistent Prayer

"With all perseverance and petition." Warfare prayer is persistent. Keep on praying. Don't quit. Don't give up (Matthew 7:7; Luke 18:1-8). On the battlefield of life we must be constantly in touch with our Commander. He speaks to us through His Word, and we speak to Him in prayer. Both lines of communication must remain open.

Intercessory Prayer

"For all the saints." The final phrase tells us for whom prayers are to be offered. Prayer is to be made for all the saints. Obviously, we can't pray for every believer by name. But we can pray for them in groupings. Believers in other nations. Persecuted saints. Suffering Christians. Isolated believers. Christians in positions of power. We need to pray for all the saints. But we also need to pray specifically for one another. Paul asks the believers to pray for him in Ephesians 6:19: "And pray on my behalf, that utterance may be given to me in the opening of my mouth, to make known with boldness the mystery of the gospel."

Paul was experiencing personally the spiritual warfare he was talking about. Spiritual warfare was no ivory-tower topic for Paul. His request for others to pray for him is evidence of the apostle's humility. Paul was a great man, but he believed that his work would be ineffective if others did not pray for him. Paul requested prayer on four other occasions: Romans 15:30-32; Colossians 4:3-4; 1 Thessalonians 5:25; 2 Thessalonians 3:1. This is a call to pray for our pastors. If Paul needed prayer, how much more do pastors and other Christian leaders need it?

Someone once asked Charles Spurgeon, "What is the secret of your ministry?"

He replied, "My people pray for me."

Prayer is a key to spiritual victory. Charlotte Elliot, who wrote the lyrics to the famous song "Just As I Am," also wrote a song titled "Watch and Pray" in 1836.

> Christian! seek not yet repose,
> Hear thy guardian angel say;
> Thou art in the midst of foes;
> Watch and pray.
>
> Principalities and powers,
> Mustering their unseen array,
> Wait for thy unguarded hours;
> Watch and pray.
>
> Gird thy heavenly armor on,
> Wear it ever night and day;
> Ambushed lies the evil one;
> Watch and pray.
>
> Watch, as if on that alone
> Hung the issue of the day;
> Pray that help may be sent down;
> Watch and pray.

100

What can I do when I'm tired of the struggle?

The epic HBO miniseries *Band of Brothers* follows a company of US paratroopers in basic training, through the invasion of Europe on D-Day, and beyond. Based on the real-life experiences of survivors, whose testimonies are sprinkled throughout the story, the series graphically portrays the heroism and suffering of men at war. The dominant character is Lieutenant Richard Winters, a strong leader who grasps his calling the way a Christian should grasp his or her calling to conflict. In one scene, after he has led his troops in a charge into battle, Winters is shown saluting an officer he has just promoted and then commenting to another soldier, "I don't like to retreat."

His classic line comes as he leads his troops into their finest moment, their stand against the Germans in the Battle of the Bulge. Overwhelmingly outnumbered, he is warned by a soldier leaving the front lines, "Looks like you guys are going to be surrounded."

Without blinking, Winters answers, "We're paratroopers, Lieutenant. We're supposed to be surrounded."

When you think about it, we should live our lives with that same mindset. We're Christians; we're supposed to contend and struggle in the good fight. Our prayer should never be to be taken out of the fight, but to embrace and celebrate the fight, for it is a fellowship, a communion with our Master and Commander who went before us. [1]

Those who know Christ have every reason to wake up each day with a positive outlook on life even in the midst of the battle. We may be surrounded, but we are on the winning side. This comforting reminder from J.C. Ryle is a reassurance to every soldier in God's army.

Let us settle in our minds that the Christian fight is a good fight—really good, truly good, emphatically good. We see only part of it yet. We see the struggle, but not the end; we see the campaign, but not the reward; we see the cross, but not the crown. We see a few humble, broken-spirited, penitent, praying people enduring hardships and despised by the world; we see not the hand of God over them, the face of God smiling on them, the kingdom of glory prepared for them. These things are yet to be revealed. Let us not judge by appearances. There are more good things about the Christian warfare than we see. [2]

Never forget that God's people fight the good fight. Someday it will be worth it all. May the prospect of what's coming tomorrow strengthen us for the battle today. May we stand strong today and every day as we look for that day.

101

A question for you:
Are you sure which side you're on?

The athletic teams of Duke University are known as the Blue Devils. Their mascot is a young man who wears a devil's suit. During one of the school's fraternity initiations, they dressed a freshman pledge in a devil suit, drove him to the edge of town after dark, and made him walk back to town.

As he was walking down the road, it started to rain. He saw a little country church, where a revival meeting was in progress. The evangelist really had the people jumping.

The boy thought, "I'll wait out the shower in the vestibule, and no one will be the wiser."

But the church didn't have any vestibule. He opened the door and stepped in—right in front of the whole congregation.

The people were already wrought up emotionally, and the sudden appearance of the devil was catastrophic. Most of them hit the back door, and quite a lot of them went through the windows. One heavyset woman sitting on the front pew surveyed the situation and saw the pileup at the back door. She knew she couldn't get through the window, so she decided to try to get out the same door the devil came in.

But the devil had the same idea, and they got stuck together in the door. Using every resource she could muster, the woman smiled at him and said, "Mr. Devil, this is the first time I've ever had a chance to meet you personally, but I want to tell you that I have been on your side all the time."[1]

That's a funny story about a very serious subject. We all must decide which side we are on in life. As we have seen, the invisible war has only two sides. You cannot remain neutral. You have to decide. You can be on the winning side by admitting your sinfulness, recognizing your need for a Savior, and transferring your trust from yourself or your good works to Jesus Christ alone as your Savior from sin. Why not take that step right now and trust Him? Don't put it off. Do it now.

The story is told that Satan once called a meeting of all the emissaries of hell and said he wanted to send one of them to help women and men ruin their souls. He asked which one wanted to go.

One demon came forward and said, "I will go."

Satan said, "If I send you, what will you tell the children of men?"

He said, "I will tell the children of men that there is no heaven."

Satan said, "They won't believe you, for there is a bit of heaven in every human heart. In the end everyone knows that right and good must have the victory. You may not go."

Then another came forward, darker and fouler than the first. Satan said, "If I send you, what will you tell the children of men?"

He said, "I will tell them there is no hell."

Satan looked at him and said, "Oh, no; they won't believe you, for in every human heart there's a thing called conscience, an inner voice, which testifies to the truth that not only will good be triumphant, but evil will be defeated. You may not go."

Then one last demon came forward, this one from the darkest place of all. Satan said to him, "And if I send you, what will you say to women and men to help them destroy their souls?"

He said, "I will tell them there is no hurry."

Satan said, "Go!" [2]

Don't be duped by the devil. Don't fall for his lie that there's no hurry. Make sure you're on the winning side by trusting Jesus Christ alone as your Savior from sin.

Notes

Introduction: Behind the *Seen*

Epigraph: C.S. Lewis, *The Screwtape Letters* (New York: Macmillan, 1961), 3.

1. Why spend time thinking about Satan and demons?

1. There are many versions of this story, and it appears to be a legend. I have found no confirmation that it's true, but it is an enlightening parable about Satan and the child of God. Some of the thoughts here are from Tony Evans, *Victory in Spiritual Warfare* (Eugene, OR: Harvest House, 2011), 11-12.

2. Ray C. Stedman, *Spiritual Warfare* (Grand Rapids, MI: Discovery House, 1999), 24-27.

3. Cited in David Jeremiah, *I Never Thought I'd See the Day!* (Nashville: FaithWords, 2011), 35-36.

4. A.W. Tozer, *Born After Midnight* (Harrisburg, PA: Christian Publications, 1959), 43.

Part One: Speak of the Devil

First epigraph: cited in John Blanchard, *The Complete Gathered Gold* (Webster, NY: Evangelical Press, 2006), 554.

Second epigraph: cited in Charles R. Swindoll, *Swindoll's Ultimate Book of Illustrations and Quotes* (Nashville, TN: Thomas Nelson, 1998), 154.

2. Does Satan really exist?

1. Paul W. Powell, *The Great Deceiver: Seeing Satan for What He Is* (Nashville, TN: Broadman Press, 1988), 11.

2. E.M. Bounds, *Guide to Spiritual Warfare* (New Kensington, PA: Whitaker House, 1984), 12.

3. C. Fred Dickason, *Angels Elect and Evil*, rev. ed. (Chicago: Moody Press, 1995), 121-22.

4. Cited in John Blanchard, *The Complete Gathered Gold* (Webster, NY: Evangelical Press, 2006), 555.

3. Is Satan a real person or just an impersonal force?

1. Cited in Craig Brian Larson and Phyllis Ten Elshof, eds., *1001 Illustrations That Connect* (Grand Rapids, MI: Zondervan, 2008), 126.

4. Where did Satan come from? How did he fall?

1. Dickason lists four points in favor of this identification:

   1. different titles—"prince" (leader) and "king"
   2. different natures—"man" (verses 2,9) and "anointed cherub" (verse 14), or "covering cherub" (verse 16)
   3. the superlatives used of the king—"full of wisdom and perfect in beauty" (verse 12)
   4. the perfection of the king—"you were blameless in your ways from the day you were created" (verse 15).

   C. Fred Dickason, *Angels Elect and Evil*, rev. ed. (Chicago: Moody Press, 1995), 136.

2. Donald Grey Barnhouse, *The Invisible War* (Grand Rapids, MI: Zondervan, 1965), 28-29.

3. Arnold G. Fruchtenbaum, *The Footsteps of the Messiah*, rev. ed. (Tustin, CA: Ariel Ministries, 2003), 560-61.

4. Erwin W. Lutzer, *The Serpent of Paradise* (Chicago: Moody Press, 1996), 29.

5. Lutzer, *The Serpent of Paradise*, 98.

5. When did Satan become Satan? When did he fall?

1. A third view, an old one that is not widely held today, posits that Satan fell between Genesis 1:1 and 1:2. This position is commonly known as the Gap or Restitution Theory. According to this view, God created a perfect creation in Genesis 1:1, and then Satan fell, and the earth was ruined and descended into chaos. Genesis 1:3-31 is viewed as the account of how God restored the world to a good state after the satanic mess was inflicted on the planet. The chief problem with this view is that one must read all of this into the text between Genesis 1:1 and 1:2. If something as monumental and devastating as cosmic rebellion occurred in this gap and led to the ruined state in Genesis 1:2, it seems strange that it would not be explicitly recorded or at least more strongly implied.

7. How is Satan related to the serpent in the Garden of Eden?

1. Henry M. Morris, *The Genesis Record* (Grand Rapids, MI: Baker Book House, 1976), 109-10.

2. B.J. Oropeza, *99 Answers to Questions About Angels, Demons and Spiritual Warfare* (Downers Grove, IL: InterVarsity Press, 1997), 91.

10. What does Beelzebub mean?

1. Robert Lightner, *Angels, Satan, and Demons* (Nashville, TN: Thomas Nelson, 1998), 74.

11. What are Satan's main activities today?

1. Tony Evans, *Theology You Can Count On* (Chicago: Moody, 2008), 592.

2. E.M. Bounds, *Guide to Spiritual Warfare* (New Kensington, PA: Whitaker House, 1984), 32.

3. John Blanchard, *Sifted Silver: A Treasury of Quotations for Christians* (Durham, England: Evangelical Press, 1995), 268.

4. Bounds, *Guide to Spiritual Warfare*, 106.

5. Erwin W. Lutzer, *The Serpent of Paradise* (Chicago: Moody Press, 1996), 120.

6. Cited in Lutzer, *The Serpent of Paradise*, 120.

12. If Jesus defeated Satan at the cross, why is he still active today?

1. John R.W. Stott, *The Cross of Christ* (Downers Grove, IL: InterVarsity Press, 1986), 231.

2. Stott, *The Cross of Christ*, 231-37.

3. David Jeremiah, *I Never Thought I'd See the Day!* (Nashville: FaithWords, 2011), 63-64.

4. Erwin W. Lutzer, *The Serpent of Paradise* (Chicago: Moody Press, 1996), 98.

5. Stott, *The Cross of Christ*, 236.

6. Stott, *The Cross of Christ*, 239-40.

13. Can Satan cause physical sickness and disease?

1. Robert Dean Jr. and Thomas Ice, *What the Bible Teaches About Spiritual Warfare*, 2nd ed. (Grand Rapid, MI: Kregel, 2000), 128-29.

17. Can Satan kill people?

1. E.M. Bounds, *Guide to Spiritual Warfare* (New Kensington, PA: Whitaker House, 1984), 99-100.

18. Can Satan control the weather?

1. D. Edmond Hiebert, *The Gospel of Mark: An Expositional Commentary* (Greenville, SC: Bob Jones University Press, 1994), 126.

19. Can Satan raise the dead?

1. Warren Wiersbe, *The Bible Exposition Commentary, New Testament*, vol. 2 (Wheaton, IL: Victor Books, 1989), 605.

2. Charles C. Ryrie, *Revelation*, in *Everyman's Bible Commentary* (Chicago: Moody Press, 1968), 83.

3. J. B. Smith, *A Revelation of Jesus Christ: A Commentary on the Book of Revelation* (Scottdale, PA: Herald Press, 1961), 195-96.

20. Is Satan omniscient—is he all-knowing?

1. Erwin W. Lutzer, *The Serpent of Paradise* (Chicago: Moody Press, 1996), 24.

23. Can Satan and demons make people sin?

1. Robert J. Morgan, *Preacher's Sourcebook of Creative Sermon Illustrations* (Nashville, TN: Thomas Nelson, 2007), 685.

2. Tony Evans, *Tony Evans' Book of Illustrations* (Chicago: Moody, 2009), 272.

24. Does Satan control and influence world leaders and nations?

1. Merrill F. Unger, *Biblical Demonology: A Study of Spiritual Forces at Work Today* (Grand Rapids, MI: Kregel, 1994), 181-82.

26. Is Satan omnipresent—is he everywhere at the same time?

1. Cited in R.C. Sproul, *Unseen Realities* (Scotland: Christian Focus, 2011), 142.

2. Sproul, *Unseen Realities*, 143.

27. Is Satan omnipotent—is he as powerful as God?

1. Robert Lightner, *Angels, Satan, and Demons* (Nashville, TN: Thomas Nelson, 1998), 66.

2. Erwin W. Lutzer, *The Serpent of Paradise* (Chicago: Moody, 1996), 102.

3. Ray Pritchard, *Stealth Attack* (Chicago: Moody, 2007), 20.

29. How does Satan gain a foothold in a person's life?

1. Cited in Robert J. Morgan, *He Shall Be Called* (New York: Warner Faith, 2005), 52.

30. How is Satan related to the occult?

1. B.J. Oropeza, *99 Answers to Questions About Angels, Demons and Spiritual Warfare* (Downers Grove, IL: InterVarsity Press, 1997), 141.

2. C. Fred Dickason, *Angels Elect and Evil*, rev. ed. (Chicago: Moody Press, 1995), 221.

31. Are UFOs the work of Satan and demons?

1. Ron Rhodes, *Alien Obsession: What Lies Behind Abductions, Sightings, and the Attraction to the Paranormal* (Eugene, OR: Harvest House, 1998), 40.

2. B.J. Oropeza, *99 Answers to Questions About Angels, Demons and Spiritual Warfare* (Downers Grove, IL: InterVarsity Press, 1997), 160-61.

33. What does "delivered over to Satan" mean?

1. John MacArthur, *Standing Strong: How to Resist the Enemy of Your Soul*, 2nd ed. (Colorado Springs, CO: David C. Cook, 2006), 39.

2. MacArthur, *Standing Strong*, 40.

3. Homer A. Kent Jr., *The Pastoral Epistles*, rev. ed. (Chicago: Moody Press, 1986), 94.

35. What is the "synagogue" of Satan in Revelation 2:9?

1. Robert L. Thomas, *Revelation 1–7: An Exegetical Commentary* (Chicago: Moody Press, 1992), 166.

39. Will the Antichrist be Satan incarnate?

1. John Phillips, *Exploring Revelation* (Neptune, NJ: Loizeaux Brothers, 1991), 166.

2. John Phillips, *Exploring the Future: A Comprehensive Guide to Bible Prophecy* (Grand Rapids: Kregel, 2003), 272.

3. Ed Hindson, *Is the Antichrist Alive and Well? 10 Keys to His Identity* (Eugene, OR: Harvest House, 1998), 8.

4. Gary Frazier, *Signs of the Coming of Christ* (Arlington, TX: Discovery Ministries, 1998), 149.

40. What is the "unholy trinity"?

1. Donald Grey Barnhouse, *Revelation: An Expository Commentary* (Grand Rapids: Zondervan Publishing House, 1971), 240.

42. Why is Satan bent on destroying the Jewish people?

1. Randall Price, "The Divine Preservation of the Jewish People," World of the Bible Ministry Update, October 1, 2009, www.worldofthebible.com/update.htm.

2. Mark Twain, "Concerning the Jews," in *How to Tell a Story, and Other Essays* (New York: The American Publishing Company, 1909), 275.

3. Arthur E. Bloomfield, *How to Recognize the Antichrist* (Minneapolis: Bethany House, 1975), 129-32.

43. When will Satan and his angels be permanently expelled from heaven?

1. John F. Walvoord, *Revelation*, rev. ed. (Chicago: Moody Press, 2011), 197.

46. When will Satan be bound in the abyss for 1000 years?

1. Kim Riddlebarger, *A Case for Amillennialism: Understanding the End Times* (Grand Rapids, MI: Baker Books, 2003), 210-11.

2. Harold W. Hoehner, "Evidence from Revelation 20," in *A Case for Premillennialism: A New Consensus*, gen. eds. Donald K. Campbell and Jeffrey L. Townsend (Chicago: Moody Press, 1992), 250.

48. Why will God release Satan from the abyss at the end of the 1000 years?

1. J. Vernon McGee, *Reveling Through Revelation* (Pasadena, CA: Thru the Bible Books, 1979), 74-75.

2. Henry Morris, *The Revelation Record* (Wheaton, IL: Tyndale House, 1983), 419-20.

Part Two: Hell's Angels

Epigraph: E. M. Bounds, *Guide to Spiritual Warfare* (New Kensington, PA: Whitaker House, 1984), 147.

50. Do demons really exist?

1. C. Fred Dickason, *Angels Elect and Evil*, rev. ed. (Chicago: Moody Press, 1995), 162-63.

51. What are demons?

1. C. Fred Dickason, *Angels Elect and Evil*, rev. ed. (Chicago: Moody Press, 1995), 174.

2. E.M. Bounds, *Guide to Spiritual Warfare* (New Kensington, PA: Whitaker House, 1984), 25-26.

52. Where do they come from?

1. Billy Graham, *Angels: God's Secret Agents*, rev. ed. (Dallas, TX: Word Publishing, 1986), 55.

56. What are the main activities of demons?

1. Ray Pritchard, *Stealth Attack* (Chicago: Moody, 2007), 15, 17.

2. Richard Thieme, "Battlespace," cited in Pritchard, *Stealth Attack*, 18.

3. W. Wayne House and Timothy J. Demy, *Answers to Common Questions About Angels & Demons* (Grand Rapids, MI: Kregel, 2011), 62.

4. J. Dwight Pentecost, *Your Adversary the Devil* (Grand Rapids, MI: Zondervan, 1969), 37.

58. Are fallen angels referred to as "the sons of God" in Genesis 6?

1. John Phillips, *Exploring Genesis* (Chicago: Moody Press, 1980), 81.

2. James Montgomery Boice, *Genesis: An Expositional Commentary*, vol. 1 (Grand Rapids, MI: Baker Books, 1998), 310.

59. What are the different ranks in the demonic hierarchy?

1. C. Fred Dickason, *Angels Elect and Evil*, rev. ed. (Chicago: Moody Press, 1995), 179.

2. John R.W. Stott, *The Message of Ephesians* (Downers Grove, IL: InterVarsity Press, 1979), 262.

3. E.M. Bounds, *Guide to Spiritual Warfare* (New Kensington, PA: Whitaker House, 1984), 89.

60. Are demons assigned to certain geographic areas?

1. Donald Grey Barnhouse, *The Invisible War* (Grand Rapids, MI: Zondervan, 1965), 132.

63. What are doctrines of demons?

1. Charles R. Swindoll, *The Church Awakening: An Urgent Call for Renewal* (Nashville, TN: FaithWords, 2010), 173. Swindoll saw the historic document in the *Yad Vashem* museum in Israel.

2. Charles R. Swindoll, *Insights on 1 and 2 Timothy, Titus* (Grand Rapids, MI: Zondervan, 2010), 82.

3. E.M. Bounds, *Guide to Spiritual Warfare* (New Kensington, PA: Whitaker House, 1984), 34.

68. Does the sixth trumpet judgment describe a human army of 200 million or a demonic one?

1. Grant R. Osborne, *Revelation*, in *Baker Exegetical Commentary on the New Testament*, ed. Moises Silva (Grand Rapids, MI: Baker Academic, 2002), 381.

2. John F. Walvoord, *The Revelation of Jesus Christ* (Chicago: Moody Press, 1966), 166, n. 13.

69. What is demon possession?

1. Alex Konya, *Demons: A Biblically Based Perspective* (Schaumburg, IL: Regular Baptist, 1990), 22.

2. Robert Dean Jr. and Thomas Ice, *What the Bible Teaches About Spiritual Warfare*, 2nd ed. (Grand Rapids, MI: Kregel, 2000), 133.

3. Dean and Ice, *What the Bible Teaches About Spiritual Warfare*, 134.

70. Does demon possession still exist today?

1. Robert Lightner, *Angels, Satan, and Demons* (Nashville, TN: Thomas Nelson, 1998), 136.

71. How can one tell the difference between mental illness and demon possession?

1. B.J. Oropeza, *99 Answers to Questions About Angels, Demons and Spiritual Warfare* (Downers Grove, IL: InterVarsity Press, 1997), 130.

72. Can a believer in Christ be demon possessed?

1. John MacArthur, *Standing Strong: How to Resist the Enemy of Your Soul*, 2nd ed. (Colorado Springs, CO: David C. Cook, 2006), 16.

2. Examples include C. Fred Dickason, *Angels Elect and Evil*, rev. ed. (Chicago: Moody Press, 1995), 207-8; and Merrill F. Unger. Unger changed his mind on this issue. In his earlier work, *Biblical Demonology*, first published in 1952, he said, "To demon possession only unbelievers are exposed; to demon influence, both believers and unbelievers…The believer, we may confidently rest assured, although perpetually faced with the subtle power and cunning of the foe from without, is shielded from the enemy within the gates." Merrill F. Unger, *Biblical Demonology* (Grand Rapids, MI: Kregel, 1994), 100. Later, based on testimony he received from missionaries around the world, Unger held that believers can be demon possessed. Merrill F. Unger, *Demons in the World Today: A Study of Occultism in the Light of God's Word* (Wheaton, IL: Tyndale House, 1971), 116-17. He reaffirmed this position in *What Demons Can Do to Saints* (Chicago: Moody Press, 1977). The reliance on stories and experience highlights the importance of staying with Scripture to define the parameters of possession by evil spirits.

3. Robert Dean Jr. and Thomas Ice, *What the Bible Teaches About Spiritual Warfare*, 2nd ed. (Grand Rapid, MI: Kregel, 2000), 134-35.

4. Mark I. Bubeck, *The Adversary* (Chicago: Moody Press, 1975), 87-88.

5. Robert Lightner, *Angels, Satan, and Demons* (Nashville, TN: Thomas Nelson, 1998), 133.

6. Dean and Ice, *What the Bible Teaches About Spiritual Warfare*, 136.

7. Dean and Ice, *What the Bible Teaches About Spiritual Warfare*, 137.

8. MacArthur, *Standing Strong*, 25.

9. Dean and Ice, *What the Bible Teaches About Spiritual Warfare*, 140.

73. Should Christians today practice exorcism or deliverance?

1. Merrill F. Unger, *Biblical Demonology: A Study of Spiritual Forces at Work Today* (Grand Rapids, MI: Kregel, 1994), 101.

2. Robert Dean Jr. and Thomas Ice, *What the Bible Teaches About Spiritual Warfare*, 2nd ed. (Grand Rapid, MI: Kregel, 2000), 146-47.

75. Can people inherit demons or generational spirits?

    1. Robert Dean Jr. and Thomas Ice, *What the Bible Teaches About Spiritual Warfare*, 2nd ed. (Grand Rapids, MI: Kregel, 2000), 202.

Part Three: The Invisible War and the Believer's "Armor All"

First epigraph: Ray C. Stedman, *Spiritual Warfare* (Grand Rapids, MI: Discovery House, 1999), 20-21.

Second epigraph: Donald Grey Barnhouse, *The Invisible War* (Grand Rapids, MI: Zondervan, 1965), 137.

78. What is spiritual warfare? Are we really in a war?

    1. Cited in Ray C. Stedman, *Spiritual Warfare* (Grand Rapids, MI: Discovery House, 1999), 71.

    2. Erwin W. Lutzer, *The Serpent of Paradise* (Chicago: Moody Press, 1996), 119.

    3. Paul W. Powell, *The Great Deceiver: Seeing Satan for What He Is* (Nashville, TN: Broadman Press, 1988), 9.

    4. Powell, *The Great Deceiver*, 1.

    5. Billy Graham, *Angels: God's Secret Agents*, rev. ed. (Dallas: Word Publishing, 1986), 59.

    6. John MacArthur, *Standing Strong: How to Resist the Enemy of Your Soul*, 2nd ed. (Colorado Springs, CO: David C. Cook, 2006), 21.

    7. Tony Evans, *Victory in Spiritual Warfare* (Eugene, OR: Harvest House, 2011), 14.

79. What is the Christian's strength for the battle against demons?

    1. Paul W. Powell, *The Great Deceiver: Seeing Satan for What He Is* (Nashville, TN: Broadman Press, 1988), 31.

    2. The SLJ Institute, "The Christian's Conflict, Ephesians 6:5-24," www.sljinstitute.net/sermons/new%20testament/pauls/pages/ephesians18.html.

80. Who are the three enemies of every Christian?

    1. James Montgomery Boice, *Genesis: An Expositional Commentary*, vol. 3 (Grand Rapids, MI: Baker Books, 1987), 912-13.

    2. Robert Dean Jr. and Thomas Ice, *What the Bible Teaches About Spiritual Warfare*, 2nd ed. (Grand Rapids, MI: Kregel, 2000), 65-66.

    3. Lewis Sperry Chafer, *Systematic Theology*, vol. 2 (Dallas: Dallas Seminary Press, 1948), 77.

    4. E.M. Bounds, *Guide to Spiritual Warfare* (New Kensington, PA: Whitaker House, 1984), 64, 75.

    5. Ray C. Stedman, *Spiritual Warfare* (Grand Rapids, MI: Discovery House, 1999), 70.

82. How do believers overcome the flesh?

    1. Ray C. Stedman, *Spiritual Warfare* (Grand Rapids, MI: Discovery House, 1999), 69-70.

    2. Robert Dean Jr. and Thomas Ice, *What the Bible Teaches About Spiritual Warfare*, 2nd ed. (Grand Rapids, MI: Kregel, 2000), 97.

83. How can we know whether temptation is coming from demons, the world, or our own flesh?

    1. Mark I. Bubeck, *The Adversary* (Chicago: Moody Press, 1975), 101.

84. Is it biblical for Christians to rebuke Satan and demons?

1. John MacArthur, *Standing Strong*, 2nd ed. (Colorado Springs, CO: David C. Cook, 2006), 89.

2. MacArthur, *Standing Strong*, 156.

85. What are binding and loosing?

1. John MacArthur Jr., *Matthew 16–23*, in *The MacArthur New Testament Commentary* (Chicago: Moody Press, 1988), 34.

87. Do territorial spirits control cities and nations, and should Christians identify and pray against them?

1. C. Peter Wagner and Rebecca Greenwood, "The Strategic-Level Deliverance Model," in *Understanding Spiritual Warfare: Four Views*, ed. James K. Beilby and Paul Rhodes Eddy (Grand Rapids, MI: Baker Academic, 2012), 179.

2. Art Moore, "Spiritual Mapping Gains Credibility Among Leaders," *Christianity Today*, January 12, 1998, 55.

3. Wagner and Greenwood, "The Strategic-Level Deliverance Model," 182-83.

4. David E. Stevens, "Daniel 10 and the Notion of Territorial Spirits," *Bibliotheca Sacra* 157: 628 (2000): 431.

5. Wayne Grudem, *Systematic Theology: An Introduction to Biblical Doctrine* (Grand Rapids, MI: Zondervan, 1995), 421.

6. Timothy Chester, *The Message of Prayer: Approaching the Throne of Grace* (Downers Grove, IL: InterVarsity Press, 2003), 231.

88. Is the intensity of spiritual warfare the same all the time?

1. Harold W. Hoehner, *Ephesians: An Exegetical Commentary* (Grand Rapids, MI: Baker Academic, 2002), 834.

2. Tony Evans, *Victory in Spiritual Warfare* (Eugene, OR: Harvest House, 2011), 93-94.

89. How do we resist the devil?

1. C. Fred Dickason, *Angels Elect and Evil*, rev. ed. (Chicago: Moody Press, 1995), 237.

90. What is the full armor of God?

1. Adapted from Ray C. Stedman, *Spiritual Warfare* (Grand Rapids, MI: Discovery House, 1999), 95-96.

2. Martyn Lloyd-Jones, *The Christian Soldier: An Exposition of Ephesians 6:10-20* (Grand Rapids, MI: Baker Books, 1977), 179.

3. David Jeremiah, *Spiritual Warfare* (San Diego, CA: Turning Point for God, 2002), 32.

91. What is the purpose of the armor of God?

1. Adapted from Ray C. Stedman, *Spiritual Warfare* (Grand Rapids, MI: Discovery House, 1999), 185-86.

93. What is the belt of truth?

1. Ray C. Stedman, *Spiritual Warfare* (Grand Rapids, MI: Discovery House, 1999), 103.

2. Steadman, *Spiritual Warfare*, 104.

94. What is the breastplate of righteousness?

1. Martin Luther, *Luther: Letters of Spiritual Counsel*, ed. and trans. by Theodore G. Tappert (Vancouver, BC: Regent College Publishing, 2003), 110.

2. Cited in Philip Graham Ryken, *The Message of Salvation* (Downers Grove, IL: InterVarsity Press, 2001), 125.

95. What are the shoes of peace?

1. Harold W. Hoehner, *Ephesians: An Exegetical Commentary* (Grand Rapids, MI: Baker Academic, 2002), 842.

96. What is the shield of faith?

1. Harold W. Hoehner, *Ephesians: An Exegetical Commentary* (Grand Rapids, MI: Baker Academic, 2002).

2. Cited in John MacArthur, *Standing Strong*, 2nd ed. (Colorado Springs, CO: David C. Cook, 2006), 137.

97. What is the helmet of salvation?

1. John MacArthur, *Standing Strong*, 2nd ed. (Colorado Springs, CO: David C. Cook, 2006), 130.

2. Ray C. Stedman, *Our Riches in Christ: Discovering the Believer's Inheritance in Ephesians* (Grand Rapids, MI: Discovery House, 1998), 378.

98. What is the sword of the Spirit?

1. James Montgomery Boice, *The Gospel of Matthew: An Expositional Commentary*, vol. 1 (Grand Rapids, MI: Baker Books, 2001), 59.

2. Boice, *The Gospel of Matthew*, 59.

99. How does prayer relate to spiritual warfare?

1. James Montgomery Boice, *Ephesians: An Expositional Commentary* (Grand Rapids, MI; Baker Books, 1997), 259.

2. John MacArthur Jr., *Ephesians*, in *MacArthur New Testament Commentary* (Chicago: Moody Press, 1986), 378.

100. What can I do when I'm tired of the struggle?

1. Adapted from Ben Patterson, *Muscular Faith* (Wheaton, IL: Tyndale Momentum, 2011), 52-53.

2. J.C. Ryle, *Holiness* (Hertfordshire, England: Evangelical Press, 1989), 62.

101. A question for you: Are you sure which side you're on?

1. Adapted from Paul W. Powell, *A Funny Thing Happened on the Way to Retirement* (Tyler, TX: Texas Baptist Leadership Center, 2000), 54-55.

2. Ben Patterson, *Muscular Faith* (Wheaton, IL: Tyndale Momentum, 2011), 76.